"About 15 years ago, I met under the aegis of Florence County fashion world, who received recruitment offers from established Hollywood stars like Loretta Young. During her years working as a model for Florence, Stephanie gained invaluable insights into 'beauty,' fashion, and modeling management. After opening my own business (Fashion Productions), I hired Stephanie as Show Director. For the next five years, she acted as my strong right arm, managing all of the vital elements of shows for prestigious charities, businesses, and fundraisers. In addition to her talent as a director, Stephanie is a fine singer and model. An attractive, down-to-earth, intelligent woman, Stephanie is supportive, dependable and visionary. I would recommend her as a knowledgeable resource for anyone in the 'beauty,' fashion, or modeling industries."

Dottie Dodd
Owner
Fashion Productions

"Stephanie has been a dear friend for many years. Her upright character makes her the ideal authoress for a book about Inner Beauty. Every woman can benefit from her insights. Stephanie's writing style unites inner and outer beauty and . . . she truly walks the talk! *How to Create Inner Beauty* will be a treasured book in my personal library."

Constance Dean Yambert
(America's Dean of Public Speaking Coaches) Owner
Constance Dean Yambert & Associates

How to Create Inner Beauty—The Secret Revealed

How to Create Inner Beauty—The Secret Revealed

Stephanie Lintz

VANTAGE PRESS
New York

Photos by Ed George, David Evans, Paul Chesley, Bruce Dale, Jodi Cobb, and Joseph H. Bailey, from the National Geographic Image Collection, on pp. 42, 43, 44, 45, 46, used by permission.

Photo by Todd Gustafson/Panoramic Images, on p. 42, used by permission.

Excerpt from "Every day is a miracle," January 25, 2002, reproduced with permission from The Life Excellence Newsletter, http://www.lifeexcellence.com.

FIRST EDITION

Published by Vantage Press, Inc.
419 Park Ave. South, New York, NY 10016

Manufactured in the United States of America
ISBN: 0-533-15412-X

Library of Congress Catalog Card No.: 2005910505

0 9 8 7 6 5 4 3 2 1

Dedication

To my husband, Bob, for helping make my dream of completing this project a reality.

To my children, Adam, Sarah, and Marymegan, the three bright lights who make my life beautiful in many ways.

To my mother, Nicki, who is always there for me and whose beauty is akin to that of a butterfly.

To Aunt Mimi, Aunt Henrietta, and Uncle Frank, in memoriam. Thank you for being great teachers of love and happiness.

To everyone who offered their support and love.

Contents

Acknowledgments

The writing of *How to Create Inner Beauty—The Secret Revealed* was a journey that began ten years ago. I am grateful to those who supported me and contributed to the successful completion of this book.

Ron Ovadia helped compile my beginning notes and edit the final draft. Lynnette Baum contributed writing and organizational skills. (Starting with my volumes of notes, outlines, and research, Lynnette guided my journey to reality in print. We have become great friends.) Connie Yambert provided support and input regarding content and writing. (Connie, my speaking coach, mentor, and special friend, has always empowered me and I am forever grateful.) Nancy, my sister and dear friend, assisted with editing, revisions and plenty of emotional support. Carol, my best friend since high school, shared insights and honesty.

Special thanks goes to my dearest Aunt Mimi, my guiding light, whose life was and is Inner Beauty made real.

How to Create Inner Beauty—The Secret Revealed

1
What Is Inner Beauty?

An Extraordinary Beauty Book

This is not an ordinary beauty book. This is a book about how to access your Inner Beauty, a beauty independent of makeup, fashion or bone structure, a beauty that affects your confidence today and your accomplishments tomorrow. This is a book about how to create "ageless" beauty, beauty that shines from within, while influencing future events and transforming dreams into realities.

As a former model, I have firsthand experience with the beauty industry. It is a thriving and prosperous part of society that has much to offer women in the areas of charm and self-care. Yet, as years passed, I was disturbed at the negative effects many wonderful women experienced when they compared themselves to perfect models. Low self-esteem was often the result, as well as a dependence upon external beauty for a sense of worth.

Surprisingly, the very models hired to represent the most well-known beauty care conglomerates also often experienced low self-esteem. I was disturbed by this fact, as I knew many of these women personally. Their struggles to understand the link between beauty and esteem inspired my research into the nature of true and lasting beauty, and its social and emotional roots. The information in this book is intended to inform and inspire, teaching every woman about her intrinsic worth and natural beauty—a beauty that cannot be duplicated, only enhanced.

Many women pair the ideas of beauty and happiness, because physical beauty may promote confidence and self-esteem. It promotes these feelings because it attracts approval from external sources, such as family, friends, and peers. While it's true that good looks can impress others and open doors for romantic relationships, lucrative jobs, and self-acceptance, at some level such co-dependent confidence feels insecure. For these doors to remain open, mastery of the Secrets of Inner Beauty must be included.

Beauty is so magnetic that watching others transform from ordinary to lovely has become a national pastime. Witness the rise in fame of popular "makeover" television shows.

During these makeover shows, normal looking women are taken to the finest beauty salons and fashion outlets, where glamour experts create a star-quality look. After this transformation, they are taken back to their families, where delight and surprise are recorded on camera.

There are many programs dealing with beauty through grooming and fashion-sense that are aired regularly on popular channels, and all of them make millions of dollars off of billions of viewers fascinated by the art of becoming beautiful. This fascination is based on the popular myth that beautiful people are happy people!

Yet, in real life, many beautiful women struggle with self-image issues. Delta Burke, star of the popular TV program "Designing Women," struggled with self-esteem after gaining weight, even though she had won many beauty pageants, including "Miss Florida."[1] Then, in her forties, she founded a chain of stores specializing in fashions for bigger beauties. These stores grew, attracting thousands of women and generating millions of dollars. Delta's 14 to 20^+ size styles generated over twenty-one million dollars in yearly retail sales.[2] These fashions flew off the shelves for one simple reason. The average American woman is size 14 or above.

In a word, Delta Burke became an icon of feminine beauty and success. But, when it came to *feeling* beautiful, was she any different from the rest of us? Delta Burke, Beauty Queen and successful entrepreneur, put it this way.

"I still have my days when I wake-up, look at myself and think, 'You are such a dog!' I still have to work hard at talking positively to myself."[3]

How many of us look in the mirror and think the same thing?

But our physical attributes provide only part of the formula for beauty.

The other part must come from within. It is our Inner Beauty and, to create and maintain Inner Beauty, positive dialogue is paramount. The following story, told by a speech instructor, is an excellent example.

"There were a lot of 'twenty-something' singles in the college class I taught on relationship-building. One woman weighed over 300 pounds yet had great self-esteem. I remember the day when an extraordinarily handsome (and available) young man joined this group of students. My three-hundred-pound friend looked at him and said, 'That's the man I'm going to marry!'

"Amused by her lofty goal, I smiled. Yet within a year, I was attending their wedding. After the ceremony,

I congratulated the bride, saying, 'How lucky that you caught such a handsome guy. . . .'

" 'What do you mean?' she replied, a spark in her eye. 'I'm the best thing that ever happened to him!' "

The moral of this story is obvious. When it comes to happiness, external beauty just isn't enough. Why? Because Outer Beauty builds self-worth on external circumstances, while Inner Beauty builds confidence on timeless principles. Inner Beauty is based on how we feel about ourselves. Only when Inner Beauty is fully developed can we achieve luminous radiance.

Statistics Never Lie

Surveys compiled by *The Washington Post* reveal startling statistics about how women feel about their looks. In 1997, 56 percent of all women surveyed disliked their outward appearance, while 66 percent were unhappy with their weight.[4]

Why, with ever expanding cosmetic lines and beauty salons to enhance our bodies, are we dissatisfied with how we look? One reason could be beauty product advertising on radio and television.

In Sal Randazzo's book, *The Myth Makers,* the power of advertising through myths and symbols is exposed.[5] This veteran of the advertising wars tells us that the primary tool used by the multibillion-dollar beauty industry is the power of stories—stories about ordinary people who better their lives by buying products that ad agencies claim will provide "The Solution" to their problems.

The ad usually starts with a "next-door-neighbor type" confronting pain or conflict to which most of us can relate. The dilemma is resolved only after a purchase of the product in the ad. The ad itself is a story in which the product provides "The Solution." If large numbers of viewers "buy" the idea, the ad is considered successful and the agency signs another twelve-month contract.

But, at what cost?

When ads end by showing women with perfect smiles, perfect bodies and perfect tans, we feel inferior, as if our human imperfections somehow diminish our worth. Think about the last time you saw a commercial for a tooth-whitening gel, or a weight-loss program, or a tanning cream. The ad always ends with the product bringing the consumer perfection. And, if they are perfect, we must be perfect, too.

My belief is that the link between the influence of "storytelling" in advertising and our perception of beauty is our thoughts. Inner dialogue is influenced by what we hear on radio and television, by what we read in newspapers and magazines, and by what we see in movies and on TV. With the rapid rise of perfectionism among women who are trying to keep pace with advertising icons, it makes sense to connect beauty product advertising to the number of women dissatisfied with their looks.

It all comes down to dollars and cents. Advertisers use storytelling to change how we think, because they know that nothing affects attitude or behavior more than our thoughts. The problem is these thoughts often translate into feelings that can become deeply rooted and dramatically affect self-image.

Through this book, you will learn how to create your own stories, and how to change and control your thoughts. Change the way you look at yourself and others will begin to see you differently, too.

The beauty you radiate from within will become the beauty that others see from without. When you create Inner Beauty you create a new way of being. Change your thoughts and you change how you see and feel, for thoughts determine the degree of Inner Beauty you experience and reveal.

Step-by-Step Beauty Guide

Throughout history, beauty has been a powerful force. Legendary beauties like Helen of Troy, Cleopatra, and Mata Hari wielded Outer Beauty like a weapon, a tool with which to amass wealth, manipulate politics and gain power. Other women, like Helen Keller and Mother Teresa, shared their Inner Beauty the same way that the sun shares light. Their radiance healed and empowered.

As a former model, experienced in a profession that deifies Outer Beauty, I can attest to the power of Inner Beauty in the real world. The information in this book was gleaned through over a decade of research. Sifting through the collected thoughts of great minds about beauty revealed one simple truth. Inner Beauty was the root of all lasting Outer Beauty. The discovery and application of the principles that sustain Inner Beauty brought me a new beginning and created a life where sharing Inner Beauty is a cherished goal.

Step-by-step, this book will take you through a process proven to access Inner Beauty while developing Outer Beauty. Follow the instructions and visualizations and a transformation of mind and body will occur in direct proportion to your efforts.

Sacred Secrets

Greek mythology recounts the tale of the Moon Spinners, goddesses who spun the light of the moon down from the heavens onto their spindles as they walked the earth at night.[6] After all the moonlight was gathered on their spindles, there would come one night with no moon, when, under cover of darkness, the sweet creatures of the earth could go their secret ways in peace, without fear of the hawk or the hunter.

That is the sacred night of safety, the night the Moon Spinners walk to the sea, the one night each month when there is no moonlight—the night before the Moon Spinners begin washing the light off of their spindles in long silver streams that unravel across the ocean toward the horizon, causing the new moon to shine again.

This myth has direct application to your growth while reading and applying the wisdom in this book, for you will be like the Moon Spinners, gathering light in ways that apply uniquely to you.

And, the secrets you glean will need to be nurtured in the secrecy of your mind and heart.

Remember the time you shared a special dream with a parent, sibling or friend, and they laughed or ridiculed your ambition? All of us have had such experiences. What happened to your hope after you received their negative feedback? The answer, for most of us, is that our desire to pursue the dream died.

Hold your dreams close to your heart. Don't talk about your plans and insights with everyone. Others may not see the worth of your dreams, because they may not be prepared to receive them. Remember not to rely on others to validate your insights. Validation, like beauty, must ultimately come from within. Create your own special nurturing environment to nourish the dreams you value.

Dreams, in their infant stages, are very vulnerable. They need special care. If cherry blossoms are exposed to frost, they do not bear fruit. If blades of grain are burned by drought, they do not bear seed. Your vision of future beauty is no less tender, especially when it is new and needs support and nurturing, instead of ridicule or criticism. Therefore, shelter your dream with secrecy. Honor it. Keep it sacred.

This may sound suspicious or unkind. Why not share the wisdom you glean with those you love? Why keep hidden your hopes for achievement and change?

Ask any savvy psychologist why, and they will probably say that many of the people we love have destroyed their dreams, burying them beneath years of self-criticism, cynicism and low self-esteem. Due to their own lack of fulfillment, they may unknowingly use words like weapons, saying to you the same cutting, unkind or even cruel things that they've said to themselves for years. They may not even be conscious of the effect their negative thoughts and words have on others, but such harshness may cripple or even halt your progress.

Remember, discovering your beauty is a journey. Inner Beauty added to Outer Beauty creates ageless beauty. This book is an opportunity to cherish the beauty that is uniquely yours.

*   *   *

2

The Seven Virtues of Inner Beauty

"If eyes were made for seeing,
Then, Beauty is its own excuse for being."[7]

—Ralph Waldo Emerson

Beauty as defined in Webster's Dictionary is, "An assemblage of graces or properties pleasing to the eye, the ear, the intellect . . . particular grace, feature, ornament or *excellence;*"[8] while Coleridge, philosopher and poet, described beauty in the Roman way, as ". . . a multitude *of virtues* in unity."[9] Yet, throughout history, beauty has been defined not only by looks, but by a combination of characteristics that create a single harmonious whole.

In the 1600's, when a woman was considered a possession, the Taj Mahal was built to honor Shah Jahan's beloved wife, Mumtaz Mahal.[10]

As a fourteen-year-old boy, Prince Khurram, the future Shah Jahan, went to a bazaar and met Arjumand Banu, age fifteen, the daughter of his father's prime minister, who sold gems at market.[11]

After purchasing a diamond from her for an exorbitant sum, the prince returned to the palace and told his father he had met his future bride. After they were wed five years later, the two were inseparable.

Though Shah Jahan had other wives, there was no

9

one he trusted more. He called her Mumtaz Mahal, or "jewel of the palace," and gave her guardianship of his royal seal, (the power to create imperial laws and authorize official documents). In return, Mumtaz devoted herself to the Emperor's welfare, riding beside him when he went to war, offering counsel regarding political issues and leading the nation in benevolent aid to his subjects.[12]

As Mumtaz lay dying while giving birth to his fourteenth child, the broken-hearted Emperor promised his wife an exquisite tomb, superior to any other on earth, a symbol of their eternal love. The Taj Mahal, the Seventh Wonder of the World, was the result.

It took seventeen years to complete the Taj Mahal. The tomb was constructed of white marble, red sandstone, jasper, jade, crystal, turquoise, sapphires, lapis-lazuli, cornelian, diamonds and other precious stones, as well as gold and precious metals, rumored to have been used as freely as common stones during construction.[13]

Millions have revered the Taj Mahal as a monument to Mumtaz and Shah Jahan's eternal love. Few have recognized it for what it is—the crowning glory of a woman possessing ageless beauty, the union of Outer Beauty, which first ignited her husband's passion, with her Inner Beauty, the radiance that fed his lifetime devotion and inspired an adoring nation.

To some women, like Mumtaz Mahal, Inner Beauty comes naturally. Other women develop Inner Beauty by mastering timeless principles. The *Seven Virtues of Inner Excellence* embody these principles. When the Seven Virtues are incorporated into our daily lives, we experience not only the benefits of the virtues themselves, but the Seven Gifts of Inner Beauty as our reward.

The Seven Gifts of Inner Beauty

The *Seven Gifts of Inner Beauty* are Peace, Self-Esteem, Power, Harmony, Strength, Compassion, and Happiness. These Seven Gifts come from mastering the Seven Virtues of Inner Excellence.

At first reading, understanding the Seven Virtues and the Seven Gifts may seem a bit overwhelming. However, the development of the virtues and gifts is a rewarding and satisfying process. Think of it as a journey of self-discovery that you travel at your own pace. Imagine yourself already in possession of these virtues and gifts and their value and power become clear.

The following list defines each of the Seven Virtues.

The Seven Virtues of Inner Excellence

1. Immaculate Work
2. Taking More Responsibility than Others
3. Punctuality
4. Cleanliness
5. Obedience to the Chain-of-Command
6. Self-Forgiveness/Forgiveness of Others
7. A Great Attitude with a Spirit of Love

Mastering the Seven Virtues creates Inner Excellence. As a result, your Inner Beauty becomes radiant and your character empowered with the Seven Gifts of Peace, Self-Esteem, Power, Harmony, Strength, Compassion and Happiness.

But Inner Excellence isn't free. We must exchange our old habits for new virtues to receive it. The following definitions of each of the Seven Virtues helps to clarify them, in both practice and power.

1. Immaculate Work

Immaculate Work means doing your job to the best of your ability until it is completely finished. And doing it with a smile! This does not mean you must slog through hours, weeks or months of misery, with a grim grin on your face. (If this describes your work, your work and your talents are not in harmony.) Immaculate Work is work that is done with love, with dedication, with every ounce of creativity. It is an inner knowledge at the end of the day that you fulfilled your responsibilities to the best of your ability.

It is easier to do Immaculate Work if your work is in tune with your talents. Once, while walking through an art fair, a friend overheard an artist say, "I am so glad I'm out here under the sky selling my art. I may only earn seven-dollars an hour, but there's not enough money in the world to make me happy working in one of those concrete boxes."

With a smile, the artist gestured toward several high-rise office buildings silhouetted against the skyline. She knew her talent, dared to use it, and did her best at it. What matters most is not how much money you earn, but the richness you feel from your work. Rich or poor, she was doing Immaculate Work, was grateful for it, and radiated Inner Beauty.

Keep in mind that Immaculate Work does not mean your work is perfect. Few can legitimately claim perfection in any field. But all of us can aspire to it, as all of us are "perfect-able."

The same notion, "perfect-able," is also true of mastering the Seven Virtues. Such mastery is not an event. It is a gradual process, like the growth of a plant, that permanently changes your lifestyle, thoughts and actions.

Clearly, Immaculate Work means, whatever your task today, you do the best you know how, even if your abilities are humble or limited by age or illness. It also means that those who possess skill and brilliance bring it all to the table, and don't hold back part. Putting all grudges, self-absorption and envy aside, they contribute at their peak, ever alert for additional ways to serve.

Let's look at the phrase "the best you know how." I have learned a miraculous lesson in my journey. As I continue to work on my mastery of the Seven Virtues, "the best I know how" keeps redefining itself. My "best" keeps getting better. Do not get discouraged if you are doing "the best you know how" and have, as yet, achieved little, if any, level of mastery. Keep working, and soon, "the best you know how" will be just the right ticket.

Immaculate Work builds healthy pride, pride that has nothing to do with competition or comparison, pride based on the sure knowledge that you did an honest day's work . . . and then some! When you return to your job two or three times, and ask, "Is this the best I can do?" you are doing Immaculate Work!

2. Taking More Responsibility than Others

Taking More Responsibility than Others requires more than merely resolving problems at home or at work. It is exercising your will. It is choosing to see things differently and change accordingly. In other words, you *choose* willingly to take responsibility, to see life from a new viewpoint, and grow. When freely accepting responsibility, we do so without resentment. Instead, we feel grateful for the opportunity to exercise our power for the benefit of others.

Think about what this means. When an argument occurs, whom do you want to blame? Anyone? Does the fault always lie with the other party? If so, why? Does blaming others free *you* from having to grow, change your behaviors or adjust your attitudes? Most people choose to stay the same, faulting others as a tool to insulate themselves from discovering new ideas and seeing themselves in new ways. Sadly, this only guarantees frustration and stagnation.

Growth is difficult because it is unsettling and painful. A classic poem describes spring as the "cruelest month," the month when the world transforms, as a rush of seedlings compete ruthlessly for life. When we are young we rush toward adulthood, wanting to grow older with passionate intensity. Yet we are more flexible, more changeable, because of our youth. We accept outside forces, like parents or authority figures, and the changes they enforce, more readily. However, as years pass, we grow older and possibly more rigid.

It's easy to be rigid. It's safe! No shocking paradigm shifts to reveal new corrections for old mistakes. No need to take the blame, feel sorry and make compensation to others. No reason to grow. However, change and adaptation are the very essence of life.

In a way, I think that criminals who are caught are extremely fortunate. For when a lawbreaker is publicly punished, he or she is afforded the opportunity to take responsibility and make retribution. If they seize this opportunity, they may change, grow and become clean, emotionally, mentally and spiritually. No more unacknowledged guilt, like excess baggage, to carry through their lives. The fact is that it doesn't matter *why* we let go

14

of our errors. The vital truth is that when we acknowledge mistakes we free ourselves to grow into someone better, stronger and truer.

At this point, you may be tempted to throw down this book and shout, "Forget it! Why should I take responsibility for everything? Others make mistakes, too. Why should I take responsibility all the time?" What you are really asking is, "What's in it for me?" Good question. What's in it for you is what you have always desired most; changeless, timeless Inner Beauty, unaffected by external circumstance.

As an example, years ago, I met a wonderful young woman named Amber. Her husband had committed adultery. During his affair, he decided to leave Amber (now pregnant) and his preschool-aged child, for the "other woman."

During the course of her divorce, Amber met "the other woman." She was shocked to discover that they looked exactly alike. Hair coloring, facial features . . . except for height, they could have been twins. During the months following her divorce, Amber sought counseling. Her counselor courageously challenged her with a totally new concept.

"What did you do," she asked, "to make him want to leave you?"

After the initial shock, Amber made a list. She was honest, even though it was painful. Amber discovered that she had treated her ex-husband in demeaning ways. Eventually, she apologized to her ex-husband and, after several years of dating, happily married another man.

There is always a good reason to rationalize our bad behavior. Amber had a great one! She could have demanded compassion and understanding, blamed her husband for the pain caused by his infidelity, not taken responsibility, and received nothing but support from her friends. But this kind of behavior robs us of the power to change, to grow to our full potential.

An acquaintance that taught speech classes at a local university also shared her story. She had a unique way of encouraging her students to change. One of the first lessons in her manual was about how to overcome resistance to growth.

"We start within our comfort zone," she said. "But circumstances rarely leave us there. Usually, something happens that shocks us with an unpleasant or uncomfortable truth. That is our moment of choice. If we choose to deny the truth that has been revealed, we immediately recycle back into our old thoughts and behaviors. But if we accept that truth, however painful, and change our behaviors, we rise to an entirely new level of maturity and achievement!"

You don't have to become a martyr, sullenly accepting blows meant for everyone around you, to develop the gifts of Inner Beauty. However, you do have to become more flexible, willing to take the initiative to recognize your own responsibility in challenging situations.

As you take more responsibility than others, you become the natural leader in any group. And your progression accelerates and improves.

3. Punctuality

Our lives are literally woven from the fabric of time. In fact, punctuality is one of the few elements of life over which we have control, because it is directly related to our actions.

I *cannot* control the actions of my spouse, my children, my family or my friends. I *can* control *my* actions and how I spend my time. This does not mean that my obligations to others, like picking my child up from school or arriving at work promptly, can be ignored or devalued. But I chose these obligations when I chose to marry or accept employment. Whatever time I have is *my* time, and *I* am responsible to master it.

In the West, many are reared to believe four myths about time. Living these myths keeps us from developing Inner Beauty.

The first myth is that *we can save time.* This is impossible. Time can only be spent, never saved. We start each day with twenty-four hours and nothing we can do will save any of it for tomorrow. The saying "Seize the Day" is based on the truth that *now* is all the time we have.

The second myth is that *others control our time.* As we buy into this myth, we encourage ourselves to feel powerless and to harbor resentment. But if we are honest, we know on some level that blaming others is just an easy way out. No matter how much of our time we spend on others, we have used our agency to make these choices in the first place.

Furthermore, there is no situation that can't be changed for the better. There are all sorts of solutions out there, and guess who is in charge of finding and implementing them? You are! Feel like everyone else gets all your time? Think up imaginative ideas that help utilize your time a bit, like sharing babysitters, taking turns carpooling to the office, exchanging labor for daycare services, taking turns doing the shopping for the week with a friend to free up your schedule for more fulfilling tasks.

The third myth is that *punctuality isn't a big deal!* After all, almost everybody is a few minutes late. So what? The big deal is that time is a multi-trillion dollar commodity. Stockbrokers make their money by trading productive "time," because the value of company stocks and shares is the result of how effectively corporate management and employees use their time. Successful problem solving, creative achievement and financial abundance are all expressions of how effectively time is put to use. Time is priceless! Because once it's gone, it can never return.

The fourth myth is that *someday we'll have more time*. This is untrue. We have all the time possible right now. We may need to increase our level of energy, improve our organizational skills or educate ourselves in time-management. These skills can be learned. The amount of time we have is fixed. It's whatever time we have today!

This reminds me of a story about a friend of mine named Gail. Gail retired and one day she told me, responding to my query about how she now uses her time, "Well, I wake up in the morning with nothing to do and by the end of the day I barely have it done."

The truths we learn from the four myths are: I can't save time, I do control my time, punctuality *is* a big deal, and I will never have more time than I have today. Remember, punctuality is within our grasp, because time is a part of life over which we *do* have a measure of control. The amount of influence we have to completely control illness, accidents, or others is limited. But we do, through discipline, control our time.

Do not choose to devalue and insult yourself or another by being late and making someone wait. Good time management nourishes your relationships with others. When you are punctual, others trust you more, your words have more value, and your authority grows.

Punctuality tells others that you mean what you say when you commit to a specific time. It causes your Inner

Excellence to shine through. Punctuality is a sign that your word can be trusted.

4. Cleanliness

Whoever came up with "cleanliness is next to godliness" got it right. There's nothing as rejuvenating as a long, hot bath. But cleanliness is more than just bathing. It is a celestial attitude that makes order and organization a joy. It is at the root of Inner Beauty, the radiant expression of health in mind and body.

Cleanliness doesn't mean that you have to be a "neat freak," insisting that every corner of your home maintain a state of perfection. In great art, there is always one area among elements of order that reflects either chaos or growth. This is necessary to keep the composition in balance. Your home may need a place or two where projects are in transition. A little chaos can benefit the soul. But just a little.

Personal cleanliness and order must be the rule.

Here's why. Cleanliness, resulting in an organized environment and body, reflects and attracts spiritual order and abundance. Possession of the virtue of Cleanliness gives you the radiance of Inner Beauty, attracting others to you through the dignity of nonverbal language that states, "I am worthy."

When you radiate Inner Beauty through cleanliness, others see you as beautiful, too. When you see someone with dirty hands, hair and skin, beauty is the last thing that they project. Cleanliness and beauty are linked as firmly as love and marriage. You can't have one without the other. And those who know the gifts of cleanliness wouldn't want it any other way.

Many religious faiths encourage cleanliness, including rites or rituals during worship that symbolize it, from baptism by sprinkling to total immersion. But cleanliness of body will be of little benefit without cleanliness of mind and heart.

Since the subject of religion has come up, let's review the purpose of the book, which is to acquire Inner Beauty. Some words that are comfortable for me, like heavenly, religion, God, faith, spirit, divine, and soul, may have different meanings to each of us. We live in a diverse world full with many faiths, belief systems, and opinions. These words are used by those of religious faith, as well as those who base their life-source on something other than religion. Whatever you believe, draw upon your own life-source to measure the meanings of these words, or any other words, in this book. Now, back to our journey.

Someone else's first impression of you may be one of admiration, but this quickly evaporates when a lovely woman uses foul language. Don't be fooled by encouragement from others to speak vulgarities. Those who get a kick out of "dirty talk" have a pack mentality, a group mentality; they are comfortable getting you to act as they act, which drags you down. The following true story illustrates this idea.

In Mexico, there is a fabulous seafood restaurant right on the beach. Out front is a large fountain filled with live lobsters. There is no mesh to enclose them, just a four-inch concrete curb.

One night, a customer asked the manager, "How do you keep the lobsters from crawling over the curb, across the beach and back to the sea?"

"Watch!" the manager replied.

After a few moments, the situation became clear. Whenever one lobster tried to crawl out of the pool, the other lobsters grabbed him and pulled him back into the pool with them. People who do wrong things drag down everyone around them. Those who habitually use unclean language have a low tolerance for those seeking a clean and organized life. They find it easier to oppose the efforts of others to grow, than to embrace change. Yet no one can possess Inner Beauty while indulging in impure communications.

The truth is that cleanliness, as a lifestyle, is an easier way to live. Without it, we end up doing everything twice, going back to complete tasks a second, third, or even fourth time, instead of following through on the first pass. Cleanliness encourages clear thinking, stimulates creativity, and makes our lives more simple and our souls more pure.

If you desire Inner Beauty and want each day to be a low-stress adventure, then incorporate cleanliness in all aspects of your life. It's a challenge, but you're up to it, or you wouldn't be reading this book!

Remember, cleanliness of mind, body and soul defines you and creates your day-to-day Inner Beauty. It is reflected in the books you read, the movies you watch, the activities you take part in, and, especially, in personal hygiene.

It feels great to snuggle between clean sheets after showering. It feels just as great when we choose uplifting resources for education and entertainment. And the rewards of cleanliness are immediate.

So start developing the virtue of cleanliness by jumping into the shower with your favorite bar of scented soap. Notice how good it feels to scrub up, to wash away dirt, bad feelings and stress. You'll love feeling clean, because feeling clean is the first step to feeling beautiful. And, *feeling beautiful will make you become beautiful!*

5. Obedience to the Chain-of-Command

Obedience to the chain-of-command is key to developing personal strength and Inner Beauty. And, the development of obedience to the chain-of-command begins within a community.

Everyone is part of a community. To survive, a community must have laws that are accepted by community members. In other words, we choose to submit to the rule of law, to protect peace, prevent chaos and promote order and prosperity.

The idea that we must keep order by maintaining obedience to the chain-of-command may sound obvious. But, free will gives everyone the option to obstruct or support the rule of law.

What may turn people off to obedience to the chain-of-command is their mistaken perception that a leader is the most important person in a group; that anyone who is not a leader is of lesser worth. This is not true.

The following story makes my point. A dear friend, Daizy, was asked to donate some of her time serving as receptionist at a fundraising office. Now, Daizy drew a good salary by working as an upper management officer of a medium-sized corporation. She had at least seventy employees under her supervision on any given day. Yet, she gladly accepted this opportunity for humble service.

What happened next was truly miraculous. Daizy performed as directed in her humble volunteer receptionist position, and, more and more, every day, enjoyed being the low person on the totem pole— "the servant." She actually enjoyed it!

People calling on the phone or stopping by the office immediately acknowledged her contribution. When anyone needed answers to questions, they went to Daizy for help.

One day, as the lunch hour came, the manager of the fundraising office signed out for lunch on one of those bulletin boards that says who's in and who's out; except, that this one had another entry, "Person in Charge." To Daizy's surprise, her name was entered on the line "Person in Charge."

All the managers had gone to lunch and left Daizy "In Charge." What a shock. It was empowering for my friend to experience how significant she was, although she had exchanged her normal duties for an otherwise entry-level responsibility. The moral of the story is that leaders are all around us. You might be one of them.

Great leaders are a combination of both compass and servant. They point toward the correct destination, lead by example and do all in their power to help family or team members reach the goal. Such a leader is focused on discovering what to do to empower followers, not on how they can reduce their options to serve.

Poor leaders enjoy being served more than serving. They think that ordering others around is part of their job. Those with such undeveloped characters habitually send someone else out for coffee, instead of honoring their workload and serving themselves.

Instead of thinking themselves above such a menial task, they would be better served by recognizing that they have two legs for a reason and their team members will work more efficiently if they are allowed to work, uninterrupted. When a leader recognizes that the team works faster and performs better when served by management, they do all they can to empower the efforts of the group, as a whole.

Follow your given leader. The importance of this one

act cannot be over-estimated. You will develop self-control, patience and faith, as you follow your leader, all attributes of an exceptionally strong character.

The universe has been designed in order, and in every situation there is an order of leadership. Avoid angering others by honoring their place in the pecking order. Remember that obedience nourishes peace, while defusing chaos. Without obedience to the chain-of-command, order would be maintained only by brute force or charisma, the lowest common denominators in society when compared with ethics and character.

Here is a story from a friend, which illustrates this virtue. My friend had a boss she didn't like. She began to rebel and was unhappy. She thought of leaving her job after ten years. She told me one day that one of her former bosses, still with the company, had given her some advice.

"Continue being yourself and don't complain," he had said. "Poor bosses never stay around long. Stay true to yourself and you will still be here when your boss is gone."

This came true for her. Be obedient to the chain of command and your Inner Beauty will shine through and you will move forward. Make obedience to the chain of command habitual.

6. Self-Forgiveness & Forgiveness of Others

It has been said that our most painful memories are the memories of futures we will never have. Many of us cling to sorrows that are extensions of "the roads not taken."

To embrace forgiveness of others, we must first forgive ourselves. This can only happen with help from the core of our being. So, whatever that is for you, include it in the following forgiveness exercises for maximum effectiveness.

Self-Forgiveness

Self-forgiveness is based on truth. Therefore, we must be willing to take a complete, fearless, penetrating inventory of our past to discover the truth about our lives.

Most of us carry too many memories—memories that cripple achievement. Carefully set aside time for your personal inventory, understanding that, through this activity, your memories may be purged and purified.

Ensure your privacy in serene surroundings. Use candles or music or incense or the sound of falling water to encourage feelings of relaxation and safety. Treat yourself gently, for this is a time for opening, for discovery, for sacred revelation, a precursor to wisdom and peace.

Keep in mind, as you review past errors, that this inventory process is no time to play the critic. Many people criticize themselves or others mercilessly. They feel that negative labels and crisp attitudes mean they are strong enough to speak the unvarnished truth. However, the truth about self-critics is that they are too weak to feel compassion, too harsh to experience empathy. Harshness is not a measuring stick for strength. Strength is measured by our ability to balance courage with consideration, and is in direct proportion to our willingness to evaluate our own weaknesses before attempting to correct others.

The fact is that the degree of criticism we exercise toward others defines the degree of mercy we exercise toward ourselves. During your self-evaluation, act as your own champion. Temper truth with tenderness and you will discover a well-spring of inner strength.

During your inventory, use a cassette player to record your observations, or write your thoughts in a diary. In your imagination, relive your past with the knowledge that you are in a safe place today, that no one and no thing can harm you. Let quiet observations rise to the surface of your mind. These observations are the insights you are meant to receive. No matter how "off" they may seem, write them down and review them later. Let yourself laugh. Let yourself cry. Let this inventory cleanse you.

When your inventory is complete, close with thoughts of thanks to your Divine Power. Allow yourself to replace all angry or condemnatory feelings toward yourself with tender understanding. Refocus from the errors of the past onto the future you *can* enjoy. Visualize yourself enjoying it. If your inventory is complete, you will feel comfortable saying, "Yes!" to the following questions.

- Is all my shame swept away?
- Do I feel delight in my future?
- Is my attitude one of, "I admit I was wrong. I'm sorry! I'll work at doing better"?
- Am I willing to make restitution to those I have hurt?
- Am I doing all I can, according to my present circumstances, to forgive myself and move on?
- Do I believe that, with the help of my Divine Power, all the difficulties of my past can be changed into blessings?
- Do I promise to do my best, trust my Divine Power and relax each day?

If you answered, "Yes!" to the previous questions, you

26

are ready to move on to the next phase: forgiving others. If not, don't worry. Take all the time you need. Since we learn by doing, our mistakes may have been piling up for a long time. Give yourself an inventory once a day, once a week or once a month, whatever time frame feels right for you, until you can honestly answer all of the above questions with a resounding, "Yes!" And, remember, self-criticism is not a virtue. Self-forgiveness is the virtue.

Forgiveness of Others

As long as we are steeped in self-hate, it is impossible to forgive others. But when forgiveness toward ourself is part of our heart and hearth, forgiving others becomes much easier.

In the previous segment on cleanliness, we canvassed the many reasons why cleanliness is essential to Inner Beauty. When we harbor resentment or refuse to forgive, it makes us unclean in our hearts. This may not sound important, but it is; because the feelings that we nourish in our hearts are the same feelings that we attract in life. Do you see how the virtues are interrelated? One virtue affects and empowers the other virtues.

Do you want relationships with happy, fulfilled, focused people? Then you must become so yourself. Do you desire friendships with well-educated, compassionate, beautiful people? Then you must develop those virtues within yourself.

The world outside of us reflects our world within. Therefore, forgiving others is not a luxury. It is a necessity.

Now that we have fearlessly reviewed and released the past, we can forgive others. Such forgiveness requires more than just thinking a good thought or two. It requires honest acknowledgment of our own responsibility, in whatever degree, for harmful events. And, to whatever extent we deem necessary, restitution for error. This requires replacing ego with humility, and, throughout the forgiveness process, focusing on positive future options, while discarding past negative events.

Forgiveness of others is a journey, not an act. There is no single event or visualization we can do to magically exchange anger or pain for forgiveness of others. Many of us have repeatedly suffered abuse, both verbal and physical, from those who will never take responsibility for their harshness nor apologize for the pain they have caused.

But their choices are not our responsibilities. How we use our will is our foremost concern.

Forgiveness of others means we say "Good-bye" to old ways of seeing things and welcome new, more positive definitions of life experiences. The following stanzas from *Comes the Dawn,* a poem written by an unknown author, best captures this concept.

So you plant your own garden and decorate your own
soul,
Instead of waiting for someone to bring you flowers.
And, you learn that you really can endure,
That you really have worth,
And, you learn . . .
That with every good-bye . . .
Comes the dawn![14]

How do we bid farewell to habits of blame and hurt and rage, embracing the virtue of forgiveness for others in their stead? Standing on the firm soil of self-forgiveness, feeling unconditional love for who we are—one by one, we offer the same to those who brought us pain, seeing them as weak and as broken as ourselves—and just as in need of charity. Sometimes, imaginary conversations with others may nourish forgiveness. Sometimes, writing letters, sealing them in bottles and tossing them into the sea may encourage forgiveness. Sometimes, just picking up the phone or scheduling time for a talk brings the forgiveness we seek.

Whatever method we use, two things must be kept in mind:

- The choices we make must be positive for everyone involved.
- The mercy we offer others is the same mercy we will receive. Not in some far off future, but now, today. The soul is an exact accountant. It pays "in" the same amount it pays "out"!

And so, we begin our journey of forgiveness, knowing it is a lifetime quest in partnership with our Divine Power. Yet no journey could be more worthwhile.

7. A Great Attitude with a Spirit of Love

Mastery of A Great Attitude with a Spirit of Love is essential in developing Inner Beauty, that inner glow that shines from truly beautiful women of any age. Attitude is an expression of how we see the world, and seeing the world through loving eyes can be our daily choice.

Each of us possesses a light that shines from within. Feed this light with positive thoughts, and attitudes become positive, even in challenging situations as our light shines even brighter.

I'm not saying that thinking you are going to grow wings will make it so. Thoughts must reflect truth, and you must believe the truths you receive. For at the core of every positive attitude is faith.

Carefully choose the truths most essential to fuel your inner glow, and focus them toward your passions. If you need a spark to get your attitude glowing, think the following inspirations, and see how you feel.

- I effortlessly receive great things every day.
- I create more Inner Beauty, moment-by-moment, hour-by-hour.
- Today, and for the rest of my life, I have an abundance of everything I need.
- My goals are easily within my reach.
- Every day, I feel love for others and love from others.
- I experience my life as peaceful and calm, regardless of my circumstances.
- I enjoy life's challenges, as obstacles encourage me to excel.
- It's as easy for me to apply the virtues of Inner Beauty as it is for me to change my shoes.
- Every setback is an excuse to slow down and enjoy my journey.
- When I make right choices, I feel great and take time to congratulate myself.
- I have the courage to know what I want and to make it happen.
- My work is my joy. My joy is my beauty.

Science has proven what philosophers have always known—that eternal laws govern the universe. The law of thought and effect is one of the most powerful. When using the law of thought to embrace a spirit of love, you are forgiving yourself, and allowing yourself to see others in a more positive light. It is definitely taking the higher path when you choose each day to have a positive attitude with a spirit of love.

See the beauty in every situation and each day will unfold strongly, with power and strength in every hour. A Great Attitude with a Spirit of Love strengthens your belief in yourself and nourishes the enormous power growing within you.

Guard the light that shines from within. No one knows how to better than you. Recognize that to realize happiness is your destiny. When you aspire to Inner Excellence, you must expect to expend more effort than those who are content with mediocrity.

Finally, seal A Great Attitude with a Spirit of Love within your heart by expressing your gratitude to others and to your Divine Power. Gratitude is an important part of maintaining a great attitude and spirit of love, and an essential element of Inner Beauty that lasts a lifetime.

When we choose gratitude, especially during times of trial, we are touched by awe at the loveliness of our lives. We are amazed by the awareness of our Divine Power. We see the precious things, the little things that make up our lives, as priceless gifts.

From the flower that sways outside the window, to the smile from a stranger on the street, to the child who looks up with eyes like our own, we feel blessed. An awareness of and gratitude for our blessings, brings softness, tenderness and love.

To feed loving feelings, write a gratitude list. Include on this list things that cannot be bought with money. From relationships to ideas to talents to opportunities; include things from nature, like the bird singing outside your door or a cloud in the sky. You will discover the many ways in which you are richly blessed. You will discover that A Great Attitude with a Spirit of Love puts you in touch with your Inner Beauty!

Mastering the Seven Virtues

But, how, while living busy, responsible lives, can we effectively master the Seven Virtues? Here are several suggestions that make mastering the Seven Virtues simple and painless.

Carry a note card in your purse or pocket with the Seven Virtues of Inner Excellence written on it. If possible, write this note card yourself. Writing an idea down changes your brain chemistry, making recall and application of ideas easier.

Your note card should include the following list:

Immaculate Work
Taking More Responsibility Than Others
Punctuality
Cleanliness
Obedience to the Chain-of-Command
Self-Forgiveness/Forgiveness of Others
A Great Attitude with a Spirit of Love

On the other side of the note card, write this sentence:

"Mastery of the Seven Virtues creates Inner Beauty!"

Below that sentence, write the Seven Gifts that accompany the Seven Virtues—Peace, Self-Esteem, Power, Harmony, Strength, Compassion, Happiness.

Read this note card every time you are stuck in traffic, sitting at a stop light, waiting in a checkout line or "on-hold" on the phone. As you do this, you continually remind your subconscious of these virtues and gifts and of their connection with Inner Beauty. Soon, your focus in all you do will target these virtues and gifts. Inner Beauty will become an unconscious habit, as natural as breathing.

Remember mastery, even imperfect mastery, of each of the Seven Virtues of Inner Excellence, automatically brings you the Seven Gifts. As you master each virtue, the power of the Seven Gifts grows exponentially. This exponential growth of the Seven Gifts peaks when all Seven Virtues are mastered.

Such mastery will change your life. It will change your looks. Many years of practicing the Seven Virtues redefined my looks as a professional model. As you progress, Inner Beauty and Outer Beauty combine to create ageless beauty. The key is the power of mastery.

The Power of Mastery

Anyone can master Inner Excellence, resulting in Inner Beauty. However, our focus must be laser-sharp for our efforts to be rewarded. Reread the definitions of the Seven Virtues. Imagine yourself enjoying the Seven Gifts. As you do so, mastering the Seven Virtues will become enjoyable, and you will experience more contentment and beauty in your life.

My journey toward mastery of the Seven Virtues, a lifetime process, began over fifteen years ago, when I became very ill. I lost weight, grew apathetic, and became very thin and weak. I had no short-term memory and could not recall how to do the simplest tasks. My body was so weak I couldn't prepare or eat food. Lifting a glass of water to my lips was almost too much for my limited strength.

Since my husband and I were separated, he brought the children by once a week during my time of illness. It was during these seemingly endless days of depression and despair, when I had no control over my health, my finances, or my family, that I received my greatest blessing. For, this was when my sweet daughter, Sarah, acted as the voice for my Divine Power.

I will never forget her words. They were always the same, and always spoken in that parting moment when, after our weekly visit, the other children had already gone to the car. That was when Sarah would snuggle against me, cling to my arm as tightly as only an eight-year-old can, look in my eyes, and, say, "Mommy, no matter what, you're going to get better! You're going to be well again. We're going to be together. I love you, Mommy! And, you're going to get better!"

She did this week after week, month after month, until her words lit a fire in my heart. That was the moment I knew my suffering had come for a reason. Not because I deserved it, and not as a random obstacle encountered by fate. But because I was of tremendous worth and my Divine Power had something extraordinary for me to learn—and something extraordinary for me to experience and share.

Inspired by my child's confidence, I researched the elemental points of health, abundance, and beauty. As I read and studied, day after day, reviewing hundreds of books, my strength improved, and I discovered something remarkable. Every truth ever recorded by man fell under one of seven categories. The categories were Immaculate Work, Taking More Responsibility than Others, Punctuality, Obedience to the Chain-of-Command,

Self-Forgiveness/Forgiveness of Others and A Great Attitude with a Spirit of Love.

Research proved that these seven categories encompassed every topic taught by the wisest minds throughout the ages. When I understood this, I realized that mastering the truths taught in these seven categories healed the soul and created Inner Beauty; hence the Seven Virtues of Inner Excellence and Seven Gifts go hand in hand to develop Inner Beauty, a beauty so rare that those who possess it are revered throughout time.

The Secret of Inner Beauty

James Gould Cozzens said, "Every day is a miracle."[15] I would change that quote to say, "Every woman is a miracle." Each woman possesses a potential for beauty far beyond mere physical good looks. Each woman has the potential for Inner Beauty locked within her heart.

This potential is realized in the flowering of her character. In other words, the more beautiful her character, the more attractive a woman is in both body and soul.

Simply put, the secret of Inner Beauty is self-mastery. Master the Seven Virtues, receive the Seven Gifts and you will cultivate Inner Beauty that is both radiant and lasting. Therefore, wherever you live, whatever you do, Inner Beauty is within your grasp.

The truth about Inner Beauty is that, without spending a cent, women who master their lives become attractive, magnetic and radiant. It is a simple secret. It is also a sacred one.

Your Sacred Secret

This sacred secret of Inner Beauty should not be shared with everyone. It is wise to protect this truth from ridicule and/or criticism. A wise man once said, "Cast not your pearls before swine."[16] The truths you learn while applying the Seven Virtues of Inner Excellence are private. They are meant for you alone. These are your pearls. Keep them secret. Keep them sacred. Keep them safe.

Do so and you will grow in self-mastery. Your reward for self-mastery is Inner Beauty.

*   *   *

3

Beauty Around the World

"With beauty before me may I walk,
With beauty behind me may I walk,
With beauty above me may I walk,
With beauty all around me may I walk . . .
In old age, wandering on a trail of beauty . . . may I
walk."[17]

—Navajo Poem

Throughout the ages, every culture in every century has
defined Outer Beauty differently. As cultures have waxed
and waned, beauty, like the Phoenix, has been reborn,
has evolved, and has continued to magically reinvent it-
self. In other words, culture has repeatedly redefined
beauty, for culture is the root from which knowledge of
Outer Beauty springs.

Each woman, like each culture, offers a unique kind
of beauty. Conversely, each culture, like each woman, re-
defines beauty in a different way.

Women, therefore, often experience dual definitions
of Outer Beauty. The first is the beauty belonging
uniquely to them, and the second is the "ideal" beauty de-
sired by the culture in which they live.

Yet, regardless of culture, women want more than a
prefabricated social "mask" of beauty. Women want age-

less beauty, beauty as unique as their fingerprints, beauty that deepens with time instead of growing dim with age. Women want Inner Beauty, and understanding culture and its influence can help us achieve Inner Beauty.

While the most common expression of "beauty" comes from the Outer Beauty that we learn from culture, each of us has another potential "beauty identity." This is our most important identity, for it is our potential to develop an Inner Beauty that is uniquely our own.

Just as the Phoenix was resurrected from burning ash, so shall your beauty be reborn through mastery of the Seven Virtues of Inner Excellence, creating Inner Beauty.[18]

"Personal beauty is a greater recommendation than any letter of introduction."[19]

—Aristotle—4th Century B.C.

Refining our Outer Beauty is a natural process. Yet mastery of the Seven Virtues of Inner Excellence is required to bring forth Inner Beauty.

Fashion and Style

Throughout my years in modeling, I realized Fashion and Style are not required to achieve Inner Beauty. Yet fashion and style are part of our culture. The clothing we wear makes a statement about the activities we choose, as well as our self-worth, status, and competence. It speaks to others in a silent language that is quickly understood and not easily withdrawn.

As explained in the book, *Individuality,* fashion is affected by environment, rank, employment, and attitude. Not surprisingly, it is also affected by architecture.

The general look of the houses, churches, and work areas around us is often mirrored in the clothing messages we both send and receive.

For example, the fashion among Greeks of the archaic period was to wear loose robes and body draping, creating a shape often used in the pillars and architecture of important buildings.[20] Gothic fashions followed the same rule. The exquisite detail found in wall tapestries, jewelry, and even furniture is easily correlated to the slender spires, arches, windows, and doors built into the cathedrals and palaces of its era.[21]

Interrelationships between fashion and architecture were also patterned throughout the Renaissance, when wadded shoulder-pads, huge sleeves, and rectangular necklines mimicked the shapes of rooms and buildings. Contemporary western fashions continued this tradition.

Our sleek, clinging styles repeat shapes commonly found in our ergonomic architecture, while their ease of use and care parallel modern society's swift modes of transport and communication.[22]

Knowledge of fashion gives us greater appreciation for the different expressions of beauty found in cultures around the world. As we broaden our understanding of the relationship between culture and beauty, the real roots of Outer Beauty become clear. These roots bring forth the definition of each culture's unique interpretation of Outer Beauty.

There is one question that never seems to go away and suggests that there must be something more to strive for than cultural expectations. "What is beauty?" The answer is Inner Beauty that is achieved by mastery of the Seven Virtues of Inner Excellence.

Now, we understand that Outer Beauty, an important expression of self within a culture, along with fashion and style, sends a clear message to others about status and power. We also understand that Inner Beauty, that divine fire that immortalizes women who possess it, nourishes and provides the Seven Gifts— Peace, Self-Esteem, Power, Harmony, Strength, Compassion, and Happiness.

Around the World

We now explore the standards of beauty created, embraced and sustained in different societies around the world. Because of the tremendous power and influence of culture, these criteria for beauty are astounding in both variety and detail.

The society in which we live determines, through culture, how we perceive beauty. It also determines how we include it in our lives. Although each culture defines beauty differently, every culture incorporates an ideal of beauty into its lifestyle.

Women in every country and every culture rejoice in making themselves as beautiful as possible. The following provides insights into how different cultures define Outer Beauty.

Beauty rituals are as essential to a healthy state of mind as they are beneficial for the body. Long before cosmetics were discovered, women were using odds and ends from nature for beauty enhancement.

It's common knowledge that African women used Shea butter as a moisturizer, that Egyptians bathed in aloe vera juice or goat's milk and that European women diminished freckles and age spots with concoctions made from elderflowers. It is also well known that Chinese women encouraged clear skin with honeysuckle, and that almost every culture used rose oil in their beauty therapies.

Walk into your kitchen and you will discover a plethora of Nature's beauty aids. Egg whites help dry oily skin. An oatmeal-honey mask refines pores. Cucumber slices reduce swelling around the eyes. Strawberries soften skin and create a vibrant complexion. Beer works wonders as a rinse for thin, flyaway hair. Countless other herbs and cooking items make great beauty aids. Throughout the ages, women have discovered such natural beauty secrets.

Beauty is a way of life for the Navajo Nation, one of many Native American Indian tribes. The Navajo word "hozho" means to go through life with balance. You live with hozho when you walk "The Beauty Way," the way of harmony between north, south, east, and west. Typical activities that nourish "The Beauty Way" involve blessings, ceremonies, traditional rituals, and daily nurturing. The most powerful expression of "The Beauty Way" is in the prayer of the Navajo.

The Navajo Night Way Ceremony

In beauty may I walk
All day long may I walk
Through the returning seasons may I walk
Beautifully, I will possess again
Beautifully birds
Beautifully joyful birds
On the trail marked with pollen may I walk
With dew about my feet may I walk
With beauty may I walk
In old age, wandering on a trail of beauty.[23]

This "Beauty Way" philosophy of the Navajo cherishes life, cherishes land, and cherishes the spirit, mind and body. Part of the "Beauty Way" is feeding one another, for it is seen as an expression of beauty that nurtures the body. Kneeling at dawn to bless the day with the pollen ceremony, then running toward the sunrise in the east, is another special way to nurture the spirit.

Culture to Culture

This young Samburu woman is radiant with confidence in her Outer Beauty. And why not? She is well on her way to becoming one of the loveliest women in her tribe. Among Samburu men, it is well known that the most desirable Samburu women have necklaces that support their chins. In other words, unless your bead necklace presses against your jaw, you have not reached the epitome of Outer Beauty.

This Japanese Maiko, an apprentice Geisha, is fifteen to twenty years of age. Because she is a Senior Maiko, her upper lip, as well as her lower lip, are partly crimson, leaving the edges of the lips white, to indicate both sensuality and rank. The white-base makeup is also applied, purposely, to leave a broad band of bare skin untouched near the hairline, to imply nudity. Because Japanese men feel about a woman's neck as American men feel about a woman's legs, the Maiko wears her hair divided in the back in the "split peach" fashion, with an erotic splash of crimson in the part and a low collar revealing her neck bones.

This beautiful woman is probably part of the fifty percent of her country's population that are descended from pure Incan blood. She wears the tall straw hat that is a tradition in Peru, with silver bangle earrings. Standards of beauty differ throughout her country, according to region. Some Peruvian women are admired for their pale complexions and Castilian descent, some for their golden skin and Aztec heritage, and others for Asian or tribal features.

Hawaiian men admire the graceful carriage and long, shining black hair of their island women. This Hawaiian beauty dances the hula, a dance created by the

Goddess Hi'iaka to tell stories through rhythmic interpretation of poetry and fable, love being the favorite topic. Hawaiian women are perceived as both powerful and mysterious, especially since myth says volumes about Hawaiian goddesses. In legend, the beauty of a Hawaiian woman is compared to the beauty of red lehua blossoms.

This veiled Banjara woman from Central Asia is at the forefront of fashion in 2004, with popular Mehndi tat-

toos on her hands and body. Her veil disguises other elements of Banjara beauty, like nose rings and/or nose jewels in both nostrils, tiny braids beside the face, embroidery, long silver earrings, tassels, silver chains, brass, gold, ivory, even animal bone, as well as coins, mirrors, cowrie shells, anklets and toe rings. Among the Banjara, fashion is directly related to both beauty and status. A single woman may wear bangles below the elbow, but only a married woman may wear bangles from shoulder to wrist.

This Chinese actress performs traditional Peking Opera in the huge three-story theatre at the Summer Pal-

ace. Her red makeup means she represents uprightness and loyalty. The Chinese word for "beauty," meaning "pleasant to the eye," is one of the first words ever found inscribed on an oracle bone in 11 B.C. But standards of beauty for Chinese women have changed radically throughout history, from slender, to stout, to delicate, to graceful. Yet, underpinning these shifting Chinese beauty preferences are the fundamentals that attract Chinese men, including education, manners, talent and virtue.

This young girl keeps herself modestly covered, a requirement to honor womanly virtue in India. Coming from a poor family, her marriage will probably be a humble one. However, the princess of India, as well as other wealthy young women, will prepare for their weddings  with the Sixteen Adornments of Woman, a series of sixteen beauty rituals corresponding to the sixteen phases of the moon. Passed down for centuries, these rituals, which bless a woman with the sixteen gifts of beauty, are as follows: her hair is oiled and ornamented, her hands and arms scrubbed with a paste of tumeric, oil and gram flower, ornaments are draped across her forehead, special cosmetics applied to her face, nose rings and earrings are put on, necklaces or garlands are hung round her neck, bangles, bracelets, armlets, rings and toe-rings slipped on (over fashionable Mehndi tattoos), and, an elaborate gold belt is fastened round her crimson sari.

Face and body paint designs, combined with spectacular feathers, make this young Huli woman beautiful  enough to outshine her friends at the annual Sing-Sing dance. Flowers, leaves, shells and beads add to her exotic attractions. Her skin glistens after she rubs it with tree oil or pig fat. If this Huli woman lives in Mendi, she will abide by local customs, and expect to wear black for her wedding and smear her body with blue-grey clay, during mourning. After

45

her marriage, she may lovingly offer hair from her head to her husband, to be woven into his ceremonial wig, a wig passed down to her sons for generations to come.

This Zuni Indian woman, from New Mexico, enjoys the beauty of heaven by wearing the exquisite silver and turquoise jewelry made by her tribe. Myth states that when the fathers of her tribe were cast down to earth,

they bit off pieces of heaven with their teeth to carry with them, to remind them of the beauty of heaven. Those bits of heaven are now the semi-precious stone, turquoise. Zuni men hunt and work the fields, while Zuni women own all familial possessions. The greatest admiration of members of the Zuni tribes is reserved for those with "k'okshi," which means "to be good, to be obedient, to be attractive." Although traditional Indian features are admired, Zuni men hold loveliness, dignity, and compassion in highest esteem.

This tribal woman smiles with confidence in her

Outer Beauty. Adorned with beads, feathers and cowries, she symbolizes the uniqueness with which each tribe's culture views beauty. Some tribal women thread their hair with gold talismans and paint their bodies ochre red, while others embellish their legs with hoops of beads, symbolic of the rolls of fat, so attractive to men in their village. Among many tribes, men prefer women so stout that they actually waddle as they walk.

Our study of cultural beauty, an ever-changing perception, has revealed a hint of something profound. For in every culture, every nation, we discovered admiration and high esteem for something beyond Outer Beauty, something beyond fashion, something beyond social norms.

Qualities like education, manners, talent, virtue, dignity, and compassion are also seen as important. Sound familiar? The Seven Virtues of Inner Excellence and Inner Beauty keep emerging around the world, culture by culture, as constant and universal truths. We now know that standards for Outer Beauty are defined differently by different cultures. This frees us to focus more on what really matters . . . the Inner Beauty that is ageless.

A Woman's Dreams and Desires

"From fairest creatures, we desire increase, that thereby beauty's rose may never die."[24]

—Shakespeare

Every woman desires to possess a beauty that is individual, lasting and complete. We want the admiration of the man we love and the knowledge that we have reached the pinnacle of our "beauty potential." The secret to nurturing Outer Beauty is Inner Beauty.

The Seven Virtues of Inner Beauty give us more than just the power to feel good about ourselves; they help us value ourselves, independent of circumstances or the opinions of others. With the Seven Virtues, we can possess a beauty that is unique and lasting. Without the

Seven Virtues, our beauty is ephemeral and temporary, dependent upon the whims of culture.

Many beautiful women experience great disappointment when they realize that Outer Beauty isn't enough. It doesn't cure low self-esteem, or make love last, or guarantee security. It doesn't prevent aging or make all of their dreams come true. The truth about Outer Beauty is that if you're not enough without it, you'll never be enough with it.

I remember how I felt when attending a fashion show. I used to say to myself, "Wow, that model is gorgeous! I could never be like that." The lesson I had to learn was that Inner Excellence creates a springboard that launches Inner Beauty. And that springboard is just the beginning!

During my ramp model training, I learned about posture, poise, grace, how to walk and turn gracefully, and how to be courageous. As I became more confident in my Outer Beauty, my mastery of the Seven Virtues of Inner Beauty helped me to change and succeed. I became a ramp model because I was drawn to the world of beauty. It intrigued and fascinated me, as well as taught me things that I believed to be truths.

Looking back, becoming a ramp model seemed such an out-of-the-box thing to do that I actually didn't think I could do it! I was middle-aged and at an emotional crossroads. It seemed like just what the doctor ordered, to refresh my self-esteem and redefine my new identity.

Being in front of hundreds of people, feeling their acceptance and acclamation, strengthened my confidence. I became secure enough to ask important questions, like, "Who decides what defines beauty?" "Can beauty be created from scratch?" "Does getting a makeover change you permanently from plain to beautiful?"

These questions came to mind as I compared my "self" with my cultural ideal of Outer Beauty. The answer came to me, clearly. The truth is that, in the end, the only ideal of beauty that really matters is our own. It is the beauty we create and admire that brings us happiness. It is the beauty we embody that creates our joy.

Life must be lived for the joy of it, not to please others or prove your worth. Believe in your Inner Beauty and it will thrive. When you feel the undertow of the cultural current dragging you toward a perception of self that is more demanding than loving, remember the following quotations.

"The thing that is really hard, and really amazing, is giving up on being perfect and beginning the work of becoming yourself."[25]

—Anna Quindlen, Newspaper Columnist

"Beauty is in the heart of the beholder."[26]

—Al Bernstein

Visualization

One way to nurture your Inner Beauty is to visualize yourself in possession of the Outer and Inner Beauty you desire. Let these visualizations remind you that Inner Beauty is fortified by Inner Excellence.

To receive the greatest benefit from the following visualizations, prepare yourself and your surroundings by creating a place where you feel relaxed and safe. Then, make sure you will not be disturbed or interrupted. When you are comfortable, repeat the following visualizations as often as you like. (And, remember, keep doing them, daily. They are easy and fun and they really work!)

Just before you relax into visualization mode, start a tape of subdued nature sound effects or mellow music. Then, with these sounds playing softly in the background, let your ideal of self (retaining all your own uniqueness) slowly grow more distinct in your mind.

Watch as your imaginary self applies the Seven Virtues successfully in difficult situations. Feel the happiness and contentment that comes from already having achieved your goal of Inner Beauty. When you feel that this exercise is complete, open your eyes, sit up, take a piece of paper and answer the following questions.

Do I believe that my Inner Beauty is within my control?

Does a woman with Outer Beauty have something I want?

What aspect of Inner Beauty will I focus on today?

Immaculate Work
Taking More Responsibility than Others
Punctuality
Cleanliness
Obedience to the Chain-of-Command
Self-forgiveness and Forgiveness of Others
Great Attitude with a Spirit of Love

Next, repeat to yourself the following affirmations. As you do so, allow yourself to feel all of the great feelings your Inner Beauty connects with now. Affirm each one.

I am beautiful in my own way.
In knowing that I do not have to be perfect to develop
     my Inner Beauty, all things become perfect.

My heart is filled with the love of beauty, so I find
  beauty wherever I go.
When I look at myself in a mirror, I see not only
  Outer Beauty, but also the beauty that shines
  from my heart.
The beauty of what I am is reflected in the beauty of
  what I do.
Everyone has beauty, and I see beauty in everyone.
My body is my temple, which houses my beauty.

This chapter began with a brief comparison of Inner
Beauty to the mythical Phoenix. In the Phoenix myth,
this magical bird flies out in front of all nations, and is the
first to view the future. The Phoenix also symbolizes re-
newal, as it dies in flames and is reborn from the heart of
its own fire.[27] When your mind is focused on Inner
Beauty, you become like the Phoenix. You see your future
beauty clearly, as less lovely thoughts and feelings are
burned away. Over time, the fire of your Inner Beauty
burns more brightly, and, as your mind is reborn, your
heart is reborn, becoming a beacon of beauty from which
your Inner Beauty shines.

*   *   *

4

Beauty American Style

"I've never seen a smiling face that was not beautiful."
—Author Unknown

America is a land of legend, an icon symbolizing freedom and financial success. Yet the very climate that encouraged our extraordinary economic opportunities also created the twenty-one billion dollar "beauty" industry. This colossal business, while creating images of "perfect" women, contributes to many of the insecurities that women have regarding their appearance.

Most women nurse an underlying doubt that, no matter what they do, no matter how much they spend, they will never look good enough to compete with the latest model, whose image is airbrushed for eight hours before being draped across a magazine cover.

So we buy truckloads of skincare products, cram our drawers with expensive makeup, pay for cosmetic surgery, and wonder, with hopeful distraction, why we still feel that, whatever we do, there's still one more thing we need.

The answer is simple. The "one more thing" we think we need is beyond the reach of those who focus on Outer Beauty.

The "one more thing" is Inner Beauty. Inner Beauty

is beauty that shines from within. And you won't find it for sale on a shelf. You'll only find it within yourself.

Inner Beauty is the quintessence of one's being. It is radiance that has its source in Inner Excellence, a loveliness that is independent of makeup, face creams or workouts.

One of my friends had an exquisitely beautiful mother. From her perfectly molded nose to her translucent skin and ideal bone structure, her face was a joy to the eye. But, without fail, this woman criticized her looks, complained about her appearance and felt that going out in public without her lipstick was a punishment to society.

This attitude affected her appearance as well as her happiness. If she had worried less about Outer Beauty and focused more on Inner Beauty, she would have experienced more of both.

So, why do we feel, with such certain passion, that we must do whatever it takes to create Outer Beauty?

Because, like generations before us, we have bought the real commodity that the multi-billion dollar "beauty" industry is selling. That commodity being a "belief" by the consumer that <u>we need that "one more thing" to achieve beauty,</u> and that, somehow, the beauty industry has it all wrapped up in a beautiful package, ready for wear.

What we don't recognize, at least not consciously, is where this message is coming from. It's coming from those glamorous, glitzy ads showing women swinging curtains of gleaming hair; showing women sauntering down sidewalks in size 1 jeans; showing women with perfect profiles, smiling at adoring men. And each woman is slipping a product into her purse, her pocket, her shopping bag.

The Myth

So what's the myth? The myth is, "You'll be beautiful after you buy this product."

So we "buy" into the myth, spending millions on beauty products and wondering which final purchase will deliver the Holy Grail of Beauty, the transformation we seek, that glow that, when released, endows every woman with radiant beauty.

Don't get me wrong, the beauty industry has made products that I love and use. These products have their place, but they fall short of the complete answer. Without Inner Beauty, all your efforts will fall short of your goal.

American women have a history of listening to that salesman, the driving force behind the million-and-one beauty products crammed onto our store shelves.

In the Old West, the Snake Oil Salesman was a common figure. He traveled by wagon, from town to town, from house to house, touting bottles of sugar water as miracle cures, promising the credulous whatever benefits they desired, from a treatment for high-baldness to a heal-all for arthritis.

The Snake Oil Salesman sold other items, as well. Items with feminine appeal, like thyme face cream and weight-loss pills.

A master con artist, the Snake Oil Salesman profited from a woman's desire for Outer Beauty, with no concern for whether or not the face creams or diet pills benefited the women who bought them. He would just move on to the next town, where he would start his pitch all over again.

I remember an old western movie. Well, not the movie, just one part of it. The town sheriff exposed the wagon-driving salesman as a fraud. The townspeople ran the Snake Oil Salesman out of town. Maybe this was the old west's version of the Food and Drug Administration, trying to protect the citizens from fraudulent products that don't work or that cause harm.

So we know the feminine obsession with Outer Beauty has a long history. From Ancient Egypt to the Renaissance to modern times, makeup, skin creams and hair dyes have enhanced a woman's Outer Beauty.

Our fixation on Outer Beauty has remained so constant and so predictable, that it is recorded in the artistic works of America's most beloved illustrator, Norman Rockwell. In the Rockwell illustration "Girl at Mirror," a teenage girl sits in a shadowy bedroom, looking at her reflection in the mirror before her. On her lap, she holds a magazine, open to a full-page photograph of Lillian Russell's face. The girl timidly touches her cheek with her free hand, her expression forlorn, the face of a child, recognizing for the first time that a cherished dream is beyond reach.

You can almost hear her thinking, "I will never be as beautiful as Lillian Russell!" Yet the undertones of Rockwell's illustration evoke a different message. For the girl is lovely, in a fresh and natural way, inspiring the viewer to observe and think: "You're beautiful, just as you are. Looking like Lillian Russell doesn't matter."

This girl's hunger for beauty is haunting. It expresses the secret yearning within all women, throughout time, for Outer Beauty. But like so many, she has missed the mark. True beauty, Inner Beauty, shines from within, and the secret to Inner Beauty is available to every woman in the world, right now.

Most attractive women recognize on some level that Inner Beauty is their deepest desire. That is why intelligent yet lovely women often receive compliments about their looks with mixed feelings of triumph and despair—for the impermanence of Outer Beauty is everpresent, and the longing for Inner Beauty cannot be denied.

One actress that personifies Inner Beauty is Julia Roberts. Look carefully at her facial features. Compared to classic beauties, her nose may be too long, her mouth too wide, her teeth too big and her forehead too broad. Yet reporters commonly describe Julia with adjectives like gorgeous, stunning and beautiful. Why? Because Julia glows from the inside out. Her Inner Beauty is so connected with her outer self, that she radiates an utterly charming attractiveness. If she had never become a movie star, Julia Roberts would still eclipse any woman's mere external beauty by simply walking into the room.

In the 1940's, when the fashion in Hollywood focused exclusively on petite performers with small, perfect features, a young actress sent her first film screen test to an L.A. director. Legend has it that this director, upon seeing her atypical, unusually large eyes during this screening, jumped up, knocked over his chair, and, shouted, "Who did that to me?" The actress was Bette Davis, and even when she was in her nineties, rock groups were still writing romantic songs dedicated to her unusually large eyes.

So what's the secret of Inner Beauty? Mastery of the Seven Virtues of Inner Excellence, which brings the Seven Gifts, as well as Inner Beauty. It's that simple.

Al Bernstein spoke truthfully when he said, "Beauty is in the heart of the beholder." He could have spoken just as truthfully by saying that beauty is in the heart of the one beheld. Valuing the beauty within each of us is easier when we strengthen our minds with positive thoughts. Use the following affirmations, and watch feelings connected with Inner Beauty, like confidence, high worth and self-esteem, increase.

Affirmations

- I see only beauty in all those who are drawn to me.
- My Inner Beauty strengthens and refreshes the best in others.
- A true renaissance of beauty is occurring in my life, today.
- From my Inner Beauty, I create.
- I accept myself, I value myself, I love myself, as I am, now.

Achieving Inner Beauty

There is a formula to achieving Inner Beauty. Like all things that last, it is simple and direct. Inner Excellence equals Inner Beauty. We may have bought the big myth about Outer Beauty in the past. Now we know the missing link in the formula for total beauty—Inner Beauty.

One not too subtle example of the "big myth" is the Cinderella story. In this tale, a poor, disinherited drudge magically morphs into the belle of the ball, revealing an Outer Beauty previously hidden beneath ashes and rags, whereupon the perfect prince begs for her hand in marriage and they live happily ever after in the castle of their choice. Was it really Cinderella's Inner Beauty, which she always possessed, that was revealed at the ball? Will this kind of fairytale romance happen to you? It is a matter of record that these types of things have happened in history.

Don't misunderstand me. It is true that Outer Beauty can affect circumstances, such as relationships, employment and income. Studies show that people with Outer Beauty actually earn 5 percent more, across the board, than those who are less attractive. But only Inner Beauty brings true happiness. Only Inner Beauty lasts.

During my modeling career, I met many women who possessed Outer Beauty, but only one with Inner Beauty as well. Her name was Dottie. I was always wondering what to do, where to set up, how to act. Dottie became my role model and mentor, as she always seemed to be "just right." Whether she knew it or not, I felt like I was under her wing.

Like so many others, Dottie was an ideal model, slender and glamorous. So why, out of twenty models, was Dottie always the center of attention? Why was she surrounded by both men and women who wanted to greet her, be near her, share in the joy of her presence?

At first, I thought it was her cheerful, professional nature. No matter how early I arrived to prepare for the ramp show, Dottie was there first, laughing and full of fun.

Then, I guessed that her attraction lay in her Immaculate Work. No matter how intense the pressure, Dottie was always poised, always the "Pro," always ready to share a smile and go the extra mile to make the event a success.

Then I surmised it was her extra effort at the end of the show, always doing more than the others, inventorying the accessories used in the show and finalizing the event. Then I thought it was her great attitude. She was one of the few models that everyone liked. I knew, immediately, there was something special about Dottie.

It wasn't until later that I experienced the strength and depth of Dottie's character. Dottie confided she had a daughter with cerebral palsy, that she got up before 5:00 A.M. each morning to bathe her, dress her and prepare her to attend a school for the mentally handicapped. Dottie weighed one hundred and twenty pounds. Her daughter was eighteen years old and weighed two hundred pounds. Only after her daughter was dressed, fed and put on the bus, did Dottie take time to think of herself.

With her glowing personality and sense of fun, I would never have guessed what she endured. She had A Great Attitude with a Spirit of Love. Dottie was the center of attention because she was radiant with Inner Beauty. She hadn't read a book or taken a course. She had simply obeyed the laws of Inner Excellence by taking the high road in life.

Never have I known a woman with such depth of character. Dottie delighted in everything, her daughter most of all. The Inner Beauty that shone from her, daily, inspired everyone who knew her. Today, Dottie is still one of the most beautiful women I have ever met.

Whatever your circumstances, whatever your opportunities, remember, Inner Beauty is within your reach. You don't have to be a model posing for a magazine, or, a royal princess, or a Hollywood icon to possess this kind of beauty. What you long for, you can create, by developing Inner Excellence. What you desire is the secret shining within . . . the secret of your Inner Beauty!

*   *   *

5

The Law of Synchronicity

"Beauty *is* putting all of yourself in harmony."[28]
—Kaylan Pickford— "Always Beautiful"

The universe is created in balanced harmonious order, an order that makes beauty a graceful, unconscious expression of nature. Take a moment to look around while in a garden or park. A bird soars with free and joyous ease. Grass grows from tree to tree, in a riot of green. Even the texture of tree bark or the shape of a leaf, if we look closely enough, may, like fine art, bring us to tears.

Everywhere, the natural world shares an abundance of beauty, as it flows with life. When this same flowing is manifest in our lives, it's called synchronicity. Synchronicity is what we experience when our lives possess harmony. When a master violinist plays her instrument or a brilliant dancer performs, they are relaxed, in sync with their song or dance, balanced, and completely harmonious. This same abundant beauty and gracious harmony may be achieved in daily life by obeying the *Law of Synchronicity.*

Before defining the **Law of Synchronicity**, it's important to understand its effects. The following story gives a clear picture of someone blessed by synchronicity and someone searching for synchronicity.

Two elderly ladies, neighbors and dear friends, saved their money to go on a cruise. At last, the day came; they bought their tickets, traveled to the port and boarded the cruise ship. Each of them had a lovely private suite, decorated with exquisite fabrics and charming furnishings. Every day, they met on deck, played games, sunned themselves and shared happy hours.

But at mealtimes, one of the ladies always excused herself and retired to her suite. The other woman enjoyed the endless array of fresh fruits and exquisitely prepared dishes, served morning, noon and night.

On the last day of the cruise, the woman who had kept to her cabin during meals said, "I wish I had had the money to afford the wonderful food you've enjoyed. My budget, after buying the ticket, left me just enough to afford cheese and crackers for the entire trip!"

"But, my friend," her companion exclaimed, guiding her toward the filet mignon, "on this cruise, all our meals are included!"

Every day, we are surrounded by glorious life opportunities. Like the "included" meals on the cruise ship, they accompany us on all our travels. Whether these opportunities flow to us effortlessly, or whether we struggle on without them, depends on how well we apply the **Law of Synchronicity**.

The **Law of Synchronicity** creates a harmonious, serendipitous pattern, a pattern that attracts abundance and supports balanced harmony, while nurturing our Inner Beauty. To enjoy the benefits of the **Law of Synchronicity**, we must understand its principles.

The first principle is the *Principle of Connectedness.*

The **Principle of Connectedness** is based on fact, not fiction. It states that everything in the universe is interconnected, in tune, in touch, because all matter in the

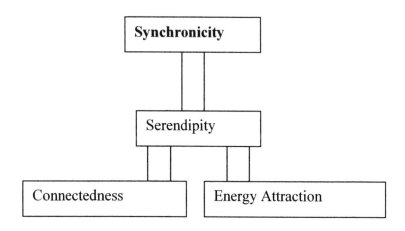

universe is made of pure energy, and all energy relates with all other forms of energy.

During the 20th century, science redefined "matter" as "energy." Solid matter that we can touch and see, like earth or water, is composed of more dense forms of energy, while the matter that creates starlight or our thoughts is composed of more refined forms of energy.

The Principle of Energy Attraction

The **Principle of Energy Attraction** means that "like" energy is attracted to "like" energy. The idea is that all matter vibrates. Different densities of matter vibrate at different rhythms.

In short, matter that vibrates at a certain rhythm is attracted to all other matter that vibrates at that same rhythm.

We are more familiar with this idea than we know. Western colloquialisms express it in phrases like, "Birds of a feather flock together," or "It takes money to make money." Whatever you *now* have, you get more of it. Wherever you are *now* at, you stay.

The Principle of Serendipity

The **Principle of Serendipity** is the capstone to the **Principles of Connectedness and Attraction**, and the final pillar supporting the **Law of Synchronicity**. It is simple, natural and experienced by almost everyone, whether they know it or not.

In fact, serendipity happens when we least expect it.

We go to the bookstore and pick up a book that falls open to a page with the information we sought. We bump into a friend who refers us to an expert who solves a problem, at just the right time.

However "lucky" serendipitous events may sound, they are not merely good fortune or coincidence. The **Principle of Serendipity** has been observed, recorded and analyzed by such well-known thinkers as Horace Walpole and Carl Jung. Carl Jung actually talked about synchronicity. The truth is that serendipity is a fact of life, and, as such, an empowering force for perfect order.

The Law of Synchronicity and You

To recap, we have learned that all matter is connected, that matter, as energy, attracts at its own level, and that serendipity is a powerful, magnetic force in life. These three basic principles support the **Law of Synchronicity**.

But, how does the **Law of Synchronicity**, that force

that creates an abundant and balanced harmonious life, the taproot for Inner Beauty, affect you? A better question is, how do you affect it? You affect it because you are in charge of it, because you control it, because you generate it. Here's how.

Your thoughts, a light and flexible form of energy, affect the vibration rate of the matter that makes up your body. As your body vibration changes, it affects the matter around it, because all matter is energy and all matter is connected. The more positive your thoughts, the more serendipity you enjoy. In femaspeak, *"As a woman thinketh, so is she"* . . . borrowed from *As a Man Thinketh, So Is He,* by James Allen.

Your thoughts bring the **Law of Synchronicity** into play. They affect the energy of the universe. They either attract or repel beauty, positive people or events, just like an invisible magnet.

And they develop a pattern, a pattern that repeats itself over and over again. Understanding this principle will transform your life.

When the *Law of Synchronicity* is active, your pattern is serendipitous; it attracts abundance and supports balanced harmony while nurturing your Inner Beauty. This is when you're in the flow, your life is going the right direction and the right opportunities keep coming your way, at the right time, over and over again. You are in the right place, in the right circumstances, 100 percent of the time.

Success is effortless—you are relaxed, certain and secure.

Best of all, you are as unaffected by external circumstances as the natural world in which you live. Like a leaf, you bend without breaking. Like a blossom, you open with synchronous ease. You are at one with nature, in harmony with the universe. Your life is a graceful, unconscious expression of natural order, allowing your radiant Inner Beauty to shine through.

Woven within the **Law of Synchronicity** is this secret. Nature is organized by design, not coincidence. The degree of Inner Beauty you express is directly linked to your awareness of and connectedness to nature's design. That is why time alone with nature develops reflection, wisdom and peace.

In nature, you must listen more, and in the silence you experience simplicity and calmness. In this way, your "Being" can become as fresh and new as nature itself. As you feel more connected to the world around you and to its intrinsic beauty, you will increase your own inner sense of "knowing." This will refresh and revitalize you and help you become more and more aligned with lasting Inner Beauty.

Nature's Wisdom

Nature is a wonderful teacher. It is timeless, ageless and boundless. The wisdom gleaned from nature falls into two main categories; the categories are **Wise Thoughts** and **Wise Feelings**.

Wise Thoughts are the insights realized when a truth bursts into the mind. **Wise Feelings** are paradigm shifts that quietly transform the emotions that determine our views.

The following are some of my favorite **Wise Thoughts:**

When you look for Inner Beauty, every day, in everything you see, Inner Beauty finds you and you embody Inner Beauty.

- Love is the habit of giving and forgetting.
- Happiness arrives with experience, but joy is a deliberate choice.
- Since I use only 10 percent of my brain, I am 90 percent undiscovered potential.
- Fear is a fantasy. Face fear and it disappears.
- Living in the present means that we laugh genuinely, with enthusiasm and generosity of spirit, and that we listen intently, as if the one we are with is the only person in the world.
- Childlike qualities are natural qualities.

Relax and respond with nature, and wisdom will descend upon you, like dew upon a leaf. Apply what you receive, and wisdom becomes like diamonds, the most precious, indestructible gems on earth.

Wise Feelings develop from healing experiences with nature. These experiences do not have to be Hollywood cliffhangers. Simple ones are often the most life changing.

A dear friend spends her nature-time with rain.

When others run from the rain, hiding indoors and complaining about the gray cloud-cover, this friend goes outside without an umbrella. She walks through the rain, face up, breathing deeply, feeling it cleanse, not just her skin, but her soul. These rain-walks change how she feels about herself and others. She returns filled with **Wise Feelings**, loving feelings, peaceful, centered, and well.

Because no two of us are the same, each of us can expect different experiences with nature. Uniqueness is a favorite expression of nature itself. After all, every tree is different, and no two flowers are alike. To refresh the garden of your soul, spend time in nature's garden, for here you will find real and profound Inner Beauty. Remember, nature is balanced and harmonious, so maintain harmony with nature. Like a breeze, let yourself pass, gentle and clean, through the forest, leaving it untouched, yet refreshed by your passing.

American Indians, during a ceremony called The Vision Quest, discover a special companion in nature, a companion that guards them and guides them through life.[29]

Like the Indians, learn from the animals, bond with those that attract you. Discover what stillness among nature and its denizens can teach. For when you are still with nature, and at one with nature you will hear new things and you will be taught in a different language.

My Aunt Mimi always said, "Don't forget to notice the beautiful flowers along your path." She meant this advice to be taken in more ways than one. Flowers are metaphors for self. There are many kinds and many varieties. All are incredibly beautiful, yet no two are alike.

Choose a flower that symbolizes your "self." Do it right now, this instant, with the first flower that crosses your mind.

This is your Sacred Flower. It means something special to you, whether you recognize what it is or not. Honor yourself by embracing this flower, by including it in special ways in your life, and you will honor yourself.

I discovered my Sacred Flower during my years of illness, and it will forever inspire me. I had been driving and decided to drive by my old home. I hadn't visited there in many months. The plumbing was bad, and one pipe was cracked on the side of the hill.

It leaked a small continuous spray of water out of the side of the garden bank and into our abandoned garden.

The garden was a ruin of blighted plants. Like tiny

headstones, blackened and broken stems thrust up every-where. Everywhere except the few inches of soil watered , non-stop, by the damaged pipe. In this tiny space, a tre-mendously huge sunflower had grown. Its massive blos-som was at least sixteen-inches wide. It thrust itself above the dead garden like a beacon of hope. At that mo-ment, I was filled with great joy; the sunflower became my favorite flower.

When Mimi said, "Don't forget to pay attention to the flowers," she meant stop and pay attention to nature.

She also meant stop and pay attention to yourself.

When we recognize the beauty of nature around us, it is easier to access our own Inner Beauty.

Sunlight has a beauty all its own. It lifts the mood, warms the body, and illuminates the world. On stormy days, when sunlight hides behind clouds, don't get de-pressed. Remember, the sun is shining just above the gray.

Once a friend took a balloon ride on a stormy day.

As long as the balloon was attached to the ground, the wind blew fiercely and the clouds roiled overhead. But after the balloon was released, it rose gently, carried tranquilly at the same speed as the wind, until it breached the cloudbank and rose into a blue sky above an ocean of white. It was more beautiful than a dream. It was a moment to be remembered.

Our journeys toward Inner Beauty are similar to this balloon ride. We may struggle during our time of prepara-tion, but, when launched onto the wind, our Divine Power will guide us toward the peace and happiness we seek.

From a practical perspective, it's smart to make sure that we take steps to keep ourselves happy, regardless of external circumstances, during our journey. If you wilt on gloomy days, install a light therapy system in your home or office. If you prefer natural methods for mood enhancement, eat less starch and sugar and spend more time exercising outdoors on sunny days. And always, always, stay focused on the blue sky waiting just above the cloud cover.

The Shadow Side of Life

Learning from the darker side of life is an essential part of discovering our Inner Beauty, for just as each rosebud casts a shadow, every lovely gift has a hidden and unseen dimension.

Think about it. As the caterpillar quietly awaits its metamorphosis, or as the starving poet awaits immortality, each, in their natural sphere, makes a tremendous contribution. Evaluate your life experiences as honestly and fairly as you assessed the shadow sides of the caterpillar and the poet. Review your past tenderly, thoughtfully. There is always some goodness to be discovered within pain and always lessons to be found in seeming disappointments.

For those who have been mistreated, this idea may sound impractical at best and impossible at worst. But the truth is that, regardless of how shadow-bound our trials or challenges, as we rise above them, we always discover Inner Beauty.

Simple as Nature

Nature is simple. Every natural element has its use and its place. Water is the cleanser, the most abundant, life-giving element on the earth. Fire is the transformer, the catalyst that, as it changes one form of matter into another, gives off heat. Earth is the nurturer. It clothes us, feeds us and provides us means for practical shelter. Air is the element of inspiration. It lifts us, carries us, raises us to a higher level.

Life is meant to be as simple as nature. Each element of life has its use and its place. The more connected we become to our Inner Beauty, the more we enjoy life, in simple, natural ways.

When we live simply and naturally, we see ourselves as intrinsically balanced, good, and holy, because our Divine Power is within us. Our spirits experience infinite boundlessness, again and again. We feel fresh, new, reborn each morning. We listen more to others and learn more as a result.

In short, a simple life is the consequence of positive thoughts. The following affirmations guide our thoughts to the natural simplicity necessary to sustain Inner Beauty.

Affirmations

- My mind is centered.
- My Divine Power goes before me each day, surrounds me, and allows each event I experience.
- My day courses onward, with perfect synchronicity.
- My body is balanced, strong, and healthy.
- I control what I am and what I do.
- I flow with the natural power within me.
- I smile and know why things are the way they are, but I tell no one. It is my secret.

- I release tension, as I see nature and refresh myself.
- The balanced harmony of nature and the universe guides me.
- In changing no one else, I am truly free.
- All things unfold naturally for my perfect good.
- My energy stays connected and in the flow, wherever I go.

Synchronicity, Harmony and Inner Beauty

Outer Beauty is at such a high premium. However, it is not enough. The quest for Inner Beauty is most important. It is a personal quest that leads to a very private victory; for each of us must connect with our Inner Beauty, ourselves.

My first conscious encounter with the **Law of Synchronicity** and Inner Beauty came when I was still struggling with illness and a rough divorce. After watching a fashion show, I walked backstage and asked to speak with the show's producer. My heart was hammering in my throat. My knees were shaking. As I walked, I almost stumbled with nervousness. Still, I followed my heart, not knowing, as I did so, where it would lead.

This striking businesswoman in her late seventies to whom I was directed introduced herself as Florence Smales. She had founded the first modeling school, as well as the first modeling agency, in Newport Beach, California.

I stepped up to her and said, "Can I model for you?"
Florence eyed me up and down.
"Walk," she said, crisply.

71

I didn't know what she meant, but I walked and turned, feeling awkward and silly.

"Call this number," she continued, handing me a slip of paper.

I went home and called it. It was a number for model training. I passed the course, re-approached Florence as a graduate, and, from that day, had as many modeling jobs from her as I wanted.

Now, this was a shock to a lot of people. Florence was hiring *me*, a greenie, over the heads of many other more experienced models. But, the **Law of Synchronicity** combined with Inner Beauty won the day. I followed my heart, started my professional modeling career, and never looked back.

You, too, can fulfill your dreams by combining the **Laws of Synchronicity** with your own personal **Inner Beauty.** Embracing the principles of Connectedness, Energy Attraction, and Serendipity is key to synchronicity.

In closing, know that balanced harmony and love are already a part of you. Allow yourself to *be, act* and *feel* natural, fresh and free, daily. Foster trust in your Divine Power; relax and let go of "controlling" tendencies. As you do, your mind and soul will become strong and healthy, your thoughts and desires will refocus with ease, and, gracefully, naturally, your Inner Beauty will begin to grow.

*   *   *

6

Women of Inner Beauty

"People are like stained-glass windows—Their true beauty is revealed only if there is a light from within."[30]

—Elizabeth Kubler-Ross

As a girl, I lived on daydreams. I would lie face-up on my bed and imagine doing grand feats. Some days, I saw myself as a scientist who discovered lifesaving medicines. On others, I was a mother, so simple and yet so complete, guiding her children to greatness. Sometimes I was even a poet who touched the hearts of millions with the wisdom of words. Yet, whatever the day, whatever the deed, I was the heroine who envisioned and achieved it.

Looking back, one idea invested each of these childhood daydreams with peculiar beauty, the idea that our greatest contributions always involved helping others.

As I matured, this idea matured, replacing self-focus with hopes for the happiness of my husband, children and friends. Yet, as I balanced support for others with self-development, I became more inspired than ever to pursue my ideal of Inner Beauty.

Throughout life, the quest for Inner Beauty draws us, like a magnet, to the same truth that thrilled my imagination as a child.

Like the North Star, it guides, attracts and enthralls.

It is not always a popular truth, but it is fascinating and eternal. The truth is this. A soul that radiates Inner Beauty is a soul surrendered to service.

As I discussed this concept of Inner Beauty with my friends, I frequently got the response, "Oh, you mean like Mother Teresa." This chapter tells the stories of many women with Inner Beauty. To honor my friends, let's begin with Mother Teresa.

Mother Teresa

From all ages and walks of life, great women arise. One of the most beloved of these is also one of the most well-known. Her name is Mother Teresa.

Christened Agnes Gonxha Bojaxhiu, the future Mother Teresa was born in Skopje, Macedonia, on August 27, 1910. When just twelve years old, Agnes felt a spiritual call to missionary work. At eighteen, she left her family and joined the Sisters of Loreto, a convocation of nuns in Ireland who sponsored several missions in India.[31]

On May 24th, 1937, the postulant, Agnes, already given the name Therese in honor of her patroness St. Therese of Lisieux, made her calling as a Loreto nun her final profession.

At this time she became known as Sister Teresa.

During her early years, she acted as instructor for St. Mary's High School in Calcutta, consumed with the task of touching and teaching the hearts of her students. Yet her selfless ardor for the welfare of others could not be contained within school walls. She was so moved by the plight of impoverished children throughout the city that she asked for permission to leave the convent school and

74

dedicate herself to laboring among the most destitute families scattered throughout the Calcutta slums.

This was the most pivotal choice of her life. She had no money, no support of any kind. She actually had to beg on the streets, as did the poor she served, for food and clothing. She never asked for transportation, but walked everywhere, putting her mission first and all other concerns second.

Through trusting in Divine Providence, the school she taught in the open air for the unkempt and unloved children of the streets became a great success. Without access to a building, desks, tables or chairs, these children learned, and both money and volunteers flowed in to support her enterprise.

Then, on October 7, 1950, the Holy See authorized Mother Teresa to start her own Order, "The Missionaries of Charity." The first concern of these devoted nuns was to "love and care for those persons nobody was prepared to look after." In 1965, Pope Paul VI decreed that the Society was an International Religious Family. Through sheer determination, fueled by faith, a woman who began her life as an anonymous girl, shared her love with poor families around the world.

Today, over 600 charitable societies and leper colonies have branched out from Mother Teresa's special Order. These groups serve the indigent in more than 123 countries, located in North America, South America, Russia, the Eastern European Bloc, Asia, Africa, Europe and Australia.

As I reflect on Mother Teresa's character, I am inspired, for although she received many awards (e.g., the Magnificent Lotus Award, the Nobel Peace Prize and the Presidential Medal of Honor) she did not work for acclaim. Mother Teresa worked for the love of the work itself, which was to improve mankind.

The Seven Virtues of Inner Beauty are embodied in Mother Teresa, including Immaculate Work, Taking More Responsibility than Others, Punctuality, Cleanliness, Obedience to the Chain-of-Command, Self-Forgiveness & Forgiveness of Others and A Great Attitude with a Spirit of Love. However, devotion to Immaculate Work nourished her life's work.

Immaculate Work means that, whatever your task, you devote yourself to it, heart and soul. What better example of Immaculate Work could we have than the life of Mother Teresa. Not content to teach students in an ordinary school, she chose to serve the poor by living with them, on their own terms, laboring ceaselessly for their support, usually on less than five hours of sleep per night.

Also known as "the saint of the gutters," Mother Teresa died in 1997, at the age of eighty-seven. There are more collections of her speeches and quotes, available on the Internet and in libraries, than most well-known public figures can boast.

One of her most memorable quotes was, "To keep a lamp burning we have to keep putting oil in it." Mother Teresa's life was a lamp of Inner Beauty, burning with a light from within.

Louisa May Alcott

Women who lift others through service are luminous. They are inspirations to all who know them or benefit from their work. One such woman is Louisa May Alcott. She has inspired young and old with high ideals for decades. Before her death, over one million of her juvenile novels were sold, and they are still popular today.

I am touched when I recall that Louisa's family nicknamed her "Louey," that she lived in a house surrounded by thirteen acres of apple orchards, and that her father chose that house because he thought apples were the perfect food. These facts open a window into her heart that makes her seem like a friend. Let's begin at the beginning.

Louisa May Alcott was born in Germantown, Pennsylvania, on November 29, 1832. Her father, Bronson Alcott, a transcendentalist philosopher and teacher, home-schooled his four daughters. The family was poor. Very poor. Yet their scholarly connections gave "Louey" a rich intellectual heritage.[32]

Louisa was welcome to browse Ralph Waldo Emerson's personal library of classical and philosophical works at any time. Every summer, Henry David Thoreau taught her botany. Mingling with the great minds of the day, like Margaret Fuller, James Russell Lowell, and Julia Ward, it's no wonder that Louisa developed a passion for women's rights and educational reform.

Yet despite these intellectual boons, life was hard for Louisa. Her brilliant, beloved father was convinced that student participation coupled with interesting lessons would promote learning, and although his advanced ideas were correct, he was a poor businessman. All of his attempts to establish schools failed.

Wearing hand-me-down clothes and thrice-turned bonnets was only the beginning of deprivation for the Alcott girls. Soon, it became clear that if bills were to be paid, the Alcott women would have to earn the money. Generously, and without blame, they got to work. Louisa herself taught school, worked as a seamstress and hired herself out as a domestic servant. This kind-hearted contribution to her family's welfare encouraged the growth of her Inner Beauty.

In the midst of poverty, at the tender age of fifteen, Louisa made a vow. "I'll be rich and famous and happy before I die, see if I won't!" Decades later, after success was assured, she confided that it was a desire to free her family from poverty that prompted this promise.

Yes, success came, but it came hard. Suffering, in the form of illness, became a tool that pruned her Inner Beauty. While acting as a nurse to wounded Civil War soldiers, "Louey" contracted typhoid fever and nearly died. Mercury poisoning from her medication, coupled with weakness in the aftermath of illness, broke her health. Yet with her vow in mind, she continued to write, trusting in hard work to reach her dream.

Louisa May Alcott wrote *Flower Fables, Hospital Sketches, On Picket Duty, Moods, The Inheritance, Under the Lilacs, Little Women, Little Men, An Old-Fashioned Girl* and many other popular works. In an age when the idea of a woman functioning outside the home was scandalous, she was a poetess, a short story writer, a nurse, a novelist and an editor.

Today, millions love Louisa May Alcott's literary works. Written from the heart, they shine with Inner Beauty. Celebrated as one of the most beloved authoresses in American literature, her collected novels, now classics, have earned many awards, including the 1993 Children's Literary Association Book Award.

Louisa's life experience is best expressed in her own words. "I am not afraid of storms, for I am learning to sail my ship."

Anne Sullivan

Another woman whose Inner Beauty strengthened her to endure the storms of life was Anne Sullivan. Described by Mark Twain as "The Miracle Worker," Anne was a pioneering teacher of the blind. She taught Helen Keller to communicate with the world, although Helen was handicapped by deafness and blindness from the age of two.[33]

Born on April 14, 1886, in Feeding Hill, Massachusetts, to a family of poor Irish immigrants, Anne Sullivan contracted trachoma and was pronounced legally blind, before she was five years old. Soon afterward, her mother died of tuberculosis.

With a foul-tempered father who drank constantly and worked inconsistently, Anne and her little brother Jimmy were passed from relative to relative. Finally, and tragically, they were abandoned to the mercy of the state poorhouse.

My heart aches when I think of these years in Anne's life; for the poorhouse, supposedly a charitable institution, was in reality a hostel for the diseased and mentally ill. Prostitutes, with ailments too vile to mention, abandoned babies who were covered with sores. Some inmates suffered from screaming delirium tremens, others from want, but all were desperate. It was a harsh and lonely place for a young girl with a little brother to grow up.

Jimmy, with his more delicate constitution and tubercular hip, couldn't endure it. Although Anne fought for them to have beds next to one another so that she could care for him, Jimmy died.

These were dark times, for Anne so dark that her only comfort was the Inner Beauty that sustained her dreams. Her most cherished dream was to get an education. During these difficult days, Anne heard of a school for the blind, a school where she could learn to read and write and become well educated. Yet, how could she, an impoverished child, qualify to attend such a school?

This crisis of thought came with ideal timing, for it was then that Frank Sanborn, Head of the Board of Charities, arrived at the poorhouse to inspect its facilities. Learning that this influential man was actually on the premises, Anne acted promptly. Waiting until Mr. Sanborn had completed his tour and was preparing to leave she literally threw herself on his mercy, begging him to send her to the blind school for an education. Impressed by her eagerness and enthusiasm, he agreed.

Anne's education at *Perkin's Institution for the Blind* began at the age of fourteen. At this school, Anne was renowned for her rebelliousness and sensitivity to correction. However, by the time she was twenty years old she had mastered her weaknesses and graduated as Valedictorian at the top of her class.

"I began to accept things as they were, and rebel less and less," Anne said. "The realization came to me that I could not alter anything but myself . . . I must bend to the inevitable, and govern my life by experience, not by might-have-beens."[34]

The Seven Virtues of Inner Beauty are embodied in this expression of Anne's maturity. Anne Sullivan began her life in horrific circumstances. She had every excuse, both poor parental example and poor circumstances, to indulge her bent toward anger and rebelliousness.

Yet she exchanged rebelliousness for obedience and became both a leader and a light!

Because Anne nourished her Inner Beauty, because she was Obedient to the Chain-of-Command, she was prepared to serve others.

At the age of twenty-one, Anne received a job offer to teach the blind and deaf child of a family living in northwest Alabama. She accepted the offer and, within four weeks of her arrival, had taught the rebellious, angry, disabled Helen Keller that the world held ideas, ideas expressed in words.

Anne taught only one child, a disabled child, a frightened, angry, rebellious child. Yet that one child bettered the lives of millions around the world. Unconsciously, Anne bears witness to the value of cultivating the virtues of Inner Beauty in the following quote.

"I have thought about it a great deal," Anne said, "and the more I think, the more certain I am, that Obedience is the gateway through which knowledge, yes, and love, too, enter the mind of the child."

Madame Curie

Women of Inner Beauty change history. Their lives stand at the threshold of great ideas and new discoveries. One woman renowned for an Inner Beauty that changed history is Madame Curie.

Born on November 7, 1867, in Poland, Marie Sklodowski, nicknamed Manya by friends and family, was raised as a patriot. Yet Warsaw, where she grew up, groaned under the iron fist of the Russian Czar, who was committed to eradicating Polish Nationalism.[35]

Because of her father's pro-Polish sympathies, he was fired by his Russian supervisor from a lucrative job as an instructor in a boys' school. Coupled with the loss of the family savings in an unwise investment, this demotion seriously affected his income. From then on, making enough money was a struggle.

I have tender feelings for Marie as a child. Her days were, more often than not, filled with fear. Because they were patriots, both she and the neighborhood children were under scrutiny by government agents. She recalls, "Constantly held in suspicion and spied upon, the children knew that a single conversation in Polish, or an imprudent word, might seriously harm, not only themselves, but also their families."

The stress of government disapproval was only the beginning of her difficulties. Her mother and her sister died, and both deaths were directly related to the poverty that oppressed her family.

Throughout these sufferings, family ties remained strong. Her father was especially attentive to the needs of his children. In the evening, by firelight, he read them classical literature, and encouraged them to become acquainted with the intricacies of his laboratory.

But the family's finances did not improve. So Marie hired herself out as a governess. Two life-changing experiences occurred during this period. The first was that Marie fell in love with the son of the family for whom she worked, and because his parents disapproved of their son's marriage to a poor girl, Marie dissolved their engagement. The second was Marie's discovery of her talent for math and the sciences.

With romance behind her and education before her, Marie moved to Paris to attend the celebrated Sorbonne University. Stories of trials, endured during her years as a student, make it clear that, in the fires of struggle, she developed her Inner Beauty.

I admire Marie's courage, especially during these challenging years. Marie was so poor that she could not afford either a warm coat or the fuel needed to warm her home; so she wore every piece of clothing she owned to keep from freezing. She was so fascinated by study that she forgot to eat the little she had, and often fainted from hunger.

Her persistence through trial brought its reward. In 1893, Marie received her Master's Degree, graduated at the top of her class, and opened a lab, with Pierre Curie, who would become her future husband. She lived to earn an astonishing nineteen degrees and fifteen gold medals, a joint Nobel Prize in Physics in 1903 and a Nobel Prize in Chemistry in 1911.

Madame Curie's radiant Inner Beauty, her dedication to serving others, is eloquently expressed in her own words. "You cannot hope to build a better world without improving individuals. To that end, each of us must work for our own improvement and, at the same time, share . . . responsibility for all humanity. . . ."

By taking more responsibility than others, Madame Curie did more than broaden the boundaries of medical science. She fueled the fires of her own Inner Beauty until she radiated that beauty across the entire world.

Helen Adams Keller

Rarely are women born with Inner Beauty. Most of us must nurture it. One woman who was famous for her Inner Beauty, who worked to develop it against all odds, was Helen Keller.

Helen Adams Keller was born on June 27, 1880, in Tuscumbia, Alabama. When she was nineteen months old, she contracted scarlet fever and was expected to die. Miraculously, Helen recovered.[36]

After Helen's recovery, her mother discovered, to her horror, that Helen had lost all sense of sight or hearing.

She could not hear the clap of a hand or see a candle passed before her eyes. In an age where physical defects were seen as character defects, Helen was both blind and deaf.

After this calamity, the family decided to treat Helen as normally as possible. As she grew, Helen became more and more a trial. Her screams and temper tantrums disrupted the household, until relatives recommended her incarceration in a mental institution.

The mental institutions of the day were commonly filthy and rat infested. Inmates were treated like animals, not people, and incarceration in such a place was tantamount to a death sentence.

In desperation, Helen's mother pleaded with Mr. Keller to find an alternative. So, as a last resort, the Kellers appealed to the management of *Perkins Institution for the Blind,* and asked them to recommend a teacher. They referred twenty-one-year-old Anne Sullivan, recent graduate and Valedictorian of their academy. She arrived soon after the Keller's initial inquiry, with few belongings but a multitude of forthright opinions.

Immediately, Anne and Helen clashed. Helen disliked her new teacher's discipline so fiercely, that she fled to anyone else in the house whenever they encountered one another. To resolve this conflict and prevent family members from interfering with Helen's training, the two were driven, by a roundabout road, to a small house on the Keller property. Their residence there was on a temporary, four-week basis. Anne Sullivan was on trial with the Keller family.

Anne had one month to establish an understanding with her disabled charge. During this month, she had to not only develop good relations with Helen, but also teach her to be well-behaved.

The young teacher felt passionately about her charge. She knew, from personal experience, that a rebellious nature was in opposition to an enlightened mind. Somewhere, deep inside the unkempt, angry Helen, Anne envisioned a soul of Inner Beauty. Yet, how could she enlighten the feelings of this sullen, rebellious child?

Anne started by teaching Helen how to keep clean. Morning and evening, she instructed her in how to wash her face and brush her hair. Throughout the day, she supervised Helen as she washed her hands and brushed her teeth.

Then, she expanded her teachings regarding cleanliness. She taught Helen to eat from her own plate, without throwing food on the floor or spilling it on her clothes. She taught her to use a napkin to keep her face and hands neat. She took Helen for long walks in the forest so that she could breathe clean air and wade in clean water.

In Anne Sullivan's philosophy, cleanliness meant little without understanding. At every opportunity, Anne tried to reach Helen's mind. She spelled words into Helen's hand, words that Helen mimicked eagerly, not knowing what they meant. Helen enjoyed the words; to her, spelling them was a game. Because she did not understand their meaning, Helen's mind was still as blind as her eyes.

As the weeks passed, Anne worked tirelessly. Slowly but surely, Helen began to learn. Yet Anne hoped and worked for more. The following quote from "The Miracle Worker," shares Anne's dream for Helen.

"I want to teach you about everything the earth is full of, everything on it that's ours for a wink and it's gone. And, what we *are* on it. The light we bring to it and leave behind in words . . . everything we know, think, feel and share . . . so that no one is in darkness or done with. . . ."[37]

But, the words repeatedly spelled into Helen's hand still meant nothing to her. So Anne continued with her rituals of cleanliness, reaching, reaching for her Inner Beauty. Miraculously, Helen learned. Now, she folded her napkin, ate neatly from her own plate and behaved normally. The family was satisfied. Anne Sullivan was not. Helen Keller's mind was blind, and Anne knew that the mind was the wellspring of Inner Beauty.

At last, the four weeks allotted for the trial period with Helen were over. In the opinion of the Kellers, the experiment was a success.

A clean, apparently tamed Helen returned home.

Yet Helen Keller's transformation, miraculous as it was, was incomplete. At the end of her four weeks of training, Anne, still spelling words at each opportunity, held Helen's hand under the water running from the spring-pump. As she did so, Anne spelled out the word "water."

Suddenly, Helen knew, for the first time, that the water running over her hand had a name. Excitedly, she began slapping other objects, demanding that their names be spelled onto her hand. For the first time in her life, she knew that words had meaning. Helen Keller was seven years old.

In her later years, Helen Keller reflected on the challenges accompanying her inability to see or hear. She said, "The best and most beautiful things in the world cannot be seen or touched, but are felt with the heart."[38] What greater expression of Inner Beauty could there be?

Helen Keller embodies the Seven Virtues of Inner Beauty. Learning and applying the virtue of Cleanliness began her quest for Inner Beauty. In fact, cleanliness was so important to Helen that, during a visit to Eaton, while recuperating from a long journey on behalf of the blind in Japan and Manchuria, a friend recorded the following story.

"Helen was in need of a quiet spot where she could be *away* from crowds for a while. Such a spot was found in an old house on the Foss Mt. Road, where the only modern convenience was running water piped in from a spring up the hill. . . .

"They did their own work. Helen made her bed, shelled peas, capped wild strawberries, and dried dishes, returning to Herbert Haas, her man-of-all-work, any plate or spoon that did not meet her fastidious standard of cleanliness. How she loved to catch him out! And how she reached out her hand to 'see' the grin on his face!

"For Herbert did it on purpose, for the fun of it."[39]

In one of Helen's most famous quotes, she said, "The public must learn that the blind man is neither genius nor freak nor idiot.

"He has a mind that can be educated, a hand which can be trained, ambitions which it is right for him to strive to realize, and it is the duty of the public to help him make the best of himself, so that he can win light through work."[40]

Helen Keller became the first blind and deaf person to graduate from college. (She graduated cum laude from Radcliffe College in 1904.) During her life, she fought for the rights of the blind and deaf, and was honored to receive such distinctive awards as Brazil's Order of the Southern Cross, Japan's Sacred Treasure, the Golden Heart from the Philippines, Lebanon's Gold Medal of Merit, as well as, America's highest honor . . . the Presidential Medal of Freedom.

In her eulogy, Senator Lister Hill paid tribute to

Helen Keller's Inner Beauty, when he said, "She will live on, one of the few, the immortal names not born to die. Her spirit will endure, as long as man can read and stories can be told, of the woman who showed the world there are no boundaries to courage and faith."[41]

Anne Frank

It is a rare soul who, like a burning torch, warms and lightens the world. Thirteen-year-old Anne Frank was one such soul. She was born June 12, 1929, in Frankfurt am Main, Germany. Anne was Jewish, and because of Nazi oppression during World War II, she and her family were forced, for two years, to hide in the attic above her father's abandoned warehouse in Holland.[42]

These were years of terror. Family, friends and strangers were approached randomly, at home, at work, in the streets, and forced into cattle cars that shipped their human cargo to death camps. There were few luxuries, as necessities became luxuries during wartime. But Anne was given a gift that she treasured more than a multitude of expensive trinkets. This gift was a diary.

This diary, her first, was given to her on her thirteenth birthday, June 12, 1942. In it she wrote, "It's the same with all my friends. I cannot bring myself to talk of anything outside the common round. Hence this diary. . . .

"I want this diary, itself, to be my friend. . . . I hope I shall be able to confide in it completely, as I have never been able to do with anyone before. I hope that it will be a great comfort to me."[43]

It *was* a great comfort to her. It was also a comfort, after its publication, to those who read it around the world.

I have often envisioned thirteen-year-old Anne, opening her new journal, looking at the unmarked pages, her pencil itching between her fingers, as if begging for her to write the words humming in her mind. Beneath her hands, these pristine pages filled up with wishes, wisdom, philosophy and wit, as she sat writing, writing in a closet-sized room, in the quiet twilight of the warehouse attic.

Anne wrote fairy tales, essays, 300 pages of notes and even started a novel, while hiding in the attic. Though she eventually became one of the most widely read young writers in the world, she did not write for fame. She wrote for self-awareness, for understanding, and to discover truth. Her writing was an expression of her Inner Beauty and it brought beauty to all.

Many of her diary entries are intimate and revealing, showing Anne as a true adolescent struggling with the fears and feelings of the young.

"My insides gnaw at me when he praises her," Anne wrote about her father's treatment of her older and prettier sister. "He doesn't notice how he treats Margot differently from me."[44]

Like other teenagers, Anne anguished over small things and large, wondered why the Nazis persecuted the Jews and longed for a peaceful world. Yet, with all her untapped brilliance, Anne did not live to see peace restored to the world. She died in a prison camp nine months after her hiding place above the warehouse attic was discovered. Yet her wonderful, loving, touching words live on in the entries of her diary.

Anne's career as a writer only extended from her thirteenth to her fifteenth year, but her Inner Beauty moved others so deeply that she will be remembered for all time. Like Anne, we may think we must do something grand to change the world, when the truth is all we need to do is be ourselves.

Today, the simple, sincere diary of Anne Frank has been translated into almost seventy languages and is one of the most widely read books in the world. The story of her life, recorded in her diary, has inspired more movies, books and awards for heroism than any single person or incident in the last century. As a testament to the remarkable Inner Beauty she possessed at such a tender age, we conclude her life story with a quotation from her famous diary. "Nobody need wait a single moment," Anne wrote, "before starting to improve the world!"[45]

I have shared these life stories of famous women, for two reasons: first, to make it clear that all great woman possess the Seven Virtues of Inner Beauty; second, to teach every woman that, regardless of her circumstances, she can cultivate these virtues; and, third, to offer encouragement, to inspire each of us with the knowledge that obstacles can not only be overcome, but transformed, into catalysts that encourage excellence, whatever our challenges.

The true stories of Mother Teresa, Louisa May Alcott, Anne Sullivan, Madame Curie, Helen Keller, and Anne Frank have always touched me. Yet, there is another woman, a great woman, whose character possesses all of the virtues of Inner Beauty, who has inspired my life more than I can express. Her name is Mimi.

My Aunt Mimi

Time is in love with some people, and one of them is the amazing, the beloved, the incomparable "Mimi." Not only is Mimi the treasured Tri-Centenarian of our family, she is my great maternal aunt.

The *Statistical Abstract of the United States* says that centenarians are one of the fastest growing groups in the American population.[46] However, there is no data on file anywhere that lists how many centenarians have actually reached 108 years of age, and lived in *three* centuries. Our dear Mimi is one of these rare centenarians.

What did Mimi do that enabled her to still be living at the ripe old age of 107? Dr. Thomas Perls, acting head of research teams at Harvard University and Beth Israel Deaconess Medical School, studied 444 families, including more than 2000 relatives of people who lived to 100 years of age. He concluded that environment and behavior are the keys to living until the centenarian years. He believes that there is an extra gene, which, after the age of 80, enables a person to reach 100 years old.

Anyone who knows Mimi knows she is 108 years young! And her youthful delight and high spirits still bring light and joy to the world! Mimi's parents, Gabriel and Belle, first met in June 1886 when Gabriel was hired to serenade one of Belle's sisters for her upcoming wedding. Little did Gabriel know, when Belle first caught his eye, that she was his soul mate and would bear him nine children.

Born on January 21, 1897, Mimi, with her sweet yet lively personality, made her own special place in the family. It is amazing to think that, just thirty-two years before she was born, President Lincoln was assassinated at the Ford Theatre; that thirty-one years before her birth, the Civil War had just ended; and, that eight years prior to her birth, the United States signed a peace treaty with the Indians. Such luminous points of history occurred astoundingly close to her birthday. Although she did not witness them, she felt their social effects first-hand.

In the wake of such stirring events, Mimi's family was living happily in Arizona. There, at the age of three, Mimi was singing two-part harmonies with her aunt. Mimi made her mark young in the form of music and other talents. Then, she contracted whooping cough at age three in 1900. But this was a minor setback that she soon overcame by her parents moving to California to save her life after the loss of her younger sister.

Mimi adored her family, an attitude that grew ever stronger during her juvenile and adult years. She became the family historian, fascinated by weddings, funerals and birth dates.

After graduating from high school in 1914, Mimi attended UCLA in Los Angeles, and graduated in UCLA's first graduating class, in 1916. To put her history in perspective, Mimi was in her twenties in the 1920's. 1915 held one of Mimi's fondest memories.

It happened when she visited the San Francisco World's Fair. Here, she heard and watched her father play in a band conducted by John Phillip Sousa. Little did she know that this was only the beginning of her celebrity encounters.

Mimi went on to meet Will Rogers, Nelson Eddy, Albert Einstein and Henry Ford. On a trip to New York with one of her sisters, Mimi even had the opportunity to audition for Oscar Hammerstein, who loved her voice.

George Washington Carver once said, "How far you go in life depends on your being tender with the young, compassionate with the aged, sympathetic with the striving and tolerant with the weak and the strong. Because, someday in life, you will have been all of these."[47]

Mimi lived this way. It was the natural expression of her Inner Beauty.

In the 1940's, Mimi's life took an unusual turn. Her sister, Evelyn, became seriously ill, so Mimi took on the guardianship of Evelyn's seven-year-old daughter, Nicki. She was, for Nicki, a surrogate mother, a role she cherished until Nicki reached adulthood.

Mimi pioneered a new archetype of the female role. In a time not far removed from the flapper era, she was a single mother with a seven-year-old child, a full-time job, and an evening job as an entertainer and singer on KFI Radio. Mimi was a 21st Century Woman, far ahead of her time.

In the 50's, when I was born, Mimi was there, compassionate, warm, affectionate and loving. Her inner-essence is still brilliant today! Of course, the first thing I recall is her singing to me. She was my champion and my guardian angel, my life teacher, showing by example what it means to love family and friends.

Mimi knew the name of every flower on God's green earth, and she had a personal relationship with everyone she met.

Mimi's beauty is ageless, because true beauty *is* ageless, timeless and immortal. Mimi is the embodiment of charity and pure love. She rejoices in life daily and her patience is endless.

Mimi taught me the joys and wonder of a large family, even though I am an only child. From her, I learned that the hallmark of a truly enlightened person is cheerfulness.

St. Augustine said, "Love is the beauty of the soul."[48] Vital, enthusiastic Mimi, embodied beauty of soul and was my exemplar for abundant living. During my growing years, her zest was contagious, and touched all who knew her. It still does. Mimi's enthusiasm brought heightened sensitivity and inspiration. She found it everywhere, in everything, and in everyone. Most of all, she found it in *herself*.

One of my childhood memories is of Mimi preparing apple turnovers for our dinner. As soon as Mimi's back was turned, I swooped down on them and ate every single one.

I couldn't honestly say I was sorry, for I loved them all! But, far more memorable than the tasty turnovers, is what happened next. Mimi came back into the room, saw that I had eaten every one of her turnovers, and gave me a big hug. She didn't mind a bit that I had snatched up those turnovers, the luscious fruits of her labors. Mimi just held me in her arms and said, "Next time, honey, you don't ever have to hide when you want something. Just tell me!" No wonder I love Mimi. . . .

Mimi never raised her voice to anyone, never spanked me, punished me or was crabby or disagreeable. She was the consummate caretaker, never asking for anything in return. A powerhouse of patience and stability, Mimi was the source of serenity that permeated her being.

Mother Teresa said, "Let no one ever come to you without leaving them better and happier."[49] This describes Mimi. Is it any wonder that Mimi is my ideal of the Seven Virtues of Inner Beauty?

My godmother, Mimi, is still cheery, lighthearted and exuberant. She has tremendous peace of mind and unshakeable centeredness.

At 108, Mimi still loves others and treats them with kindness, honor and dignity. She has gone from riding on horse-drawn wagons to flying in planes, and has loved every minute of the trip.

The well-known speaker, Wayne Dyer, said, "Self-worth comes from one thing—thinking that you are worthy." He also said, "What comes out of you when you are squeezed is what is inside of you."[50]

Throughout her life, Mimi loved herself, which made it easy for her to love others, even when she was under pressure. So, she served others cheerfully. One night, it was storming outside. As Mimi looked down on me, snuggled comfortably in my pajamas, I remember her saying, "We're going to Viola Hartnack's, to bring her some soup."

When you're small, you don't question the logic of driving across town in the pouring rain with a jar of soup. As I have matured, the many acts of charity that I witnessed from Mimi testified that kindness was her credo.

Vincent Van Gogh said, "It is good to love many things, for therein lies true strength; whosoever loves much, performs and can accomplish much . . . and what is done in love, is well done."[51] That single sentence describes Mimi to a T.

Although Mimi never married, her devotion to family binding her more strongly than any romance, she had her share of sweethearts. In her 90's, she met two great men who were devoted to her and loved her with all of their hearts. One of them was Jack, a jazz pianist. The other was David, a suitor she saw daily. Mimi delighted in their company and treasured their friendship.

Mimi is still an incredible role model. She has aged gracefully and joyfully. In my mind, Mimi is the eighth wonder of the world! When asked about her life, its challenges and limitations, she always smiles and says, "I haven't missed a thing!" At age ninety-seven, she even wrote a book about her life.

I wanted to introduce you to Mimi, because she is one of the great women of the world. Her life was and is Inner

Beauty made real. Mentioning her in this book is my way of acknowledging her courage and light, leading the way, by example, for others to follow. She was never famous, or given medals or awards. Her greatness was in her speaking directly to the heart of the matter—true and ageless beauty—Inner Beauty.

Women of Inner Beauty share their love for the joy of it. Generously, kindly, they simply live, and their lives make the world a better place. As you develop the Seven Virtues of Inner Beauty, you, too, will experience a change of heart. Life will become more vibrant. Love will become more abundant. You will know that just being yourself is a great gift, a gift that lifts the lives of others and makes the world a better, brighter, more beautiful place.

*   *   *

7

Inner Beauty—A Gift or a Goal?

Where shall you seek beauty, and how shall you find her,
Unless, she, herself, be your way and your guide?
Beauty is eternity gazing at itself in a mirror.
But, you are eternity and you are the mirror.[52]

—Kahlil Gibran

Life is filled with beauty! I challenge every woman to bring her unique Inner Beauty to life. Like looking in a mirror, living a life based on Inner Beauty shows us who we are. Still, when we seek Inner Beauty, we experience more than a reflection of self. Instead, we experience a discovery of self.

As we discover more about our Inner Beauty, it grows more radiant, and we understand the Seven Virtues more completely. Using the Seven Virtues as our guide, we choose not to be affected by circumstances or distractions.

Instead, we focus on increasing our happiness, and the happiness of others, by sharing our Inner Beauty. As we do, we learn that repetition brings mastery. The Seven Virtues become habits, easy to incorporate, and enjoyable to live.

Inner Beauty keeps us on track. It hones and refines our vision until we see what is clearly most important in each situation. When our lives are filled with Inner Beauty, we are relaxed, calm, intuitive, and constantly cognizant of the inexpressible worth of self and others. We habitually put aside commonplace events in exchange for moments of appreciation. We feel in awe of creation, thrilled by the grandeur of the stars, while touched by the perfection of a simple flower.

During our early years, especially school years, we are most likely to be unconscious of our Inner Beauty. We spend this time focusing on our culture's ideal of Outer Beauty. We struggle to combine our unique Outer Beauty with our culture's universal recipe for beauty. This struggle may suppress our growth of Inner Beauty, that inner glow, the spark of inward fire, which will eventually emerge as we develop our Inner Beauty. Only as we master the Seven Virtues will we give birth to our Inner Beauty. And, as we continue in the mastery of this process, our Inner Beauty will become more and more powerful.

Too often, we miss this vital knowledge. Somehow, we focus our efforts at excellence on creating a frizz-free hairstyle or on buying an ideal wardrobe. If, however, we could wave a magic wand, most of us would conjure more noble powers, powers that, if we dared, we could access, today, through the development of our Inner Beauty.

The Beauty Debate

The value of beauty was the subject of debate during the fifth century, when Socrates declared, "Beauty is a short-lived tyranny."[53] However, since Socrates, an unattractive man, was born into a culture that deified Outer Beauty, his perspective may have had spin from an attitude of "sour grapes."

Yet, throughout the ages, the Beauty Debate has continued.

As centuries passed, different interpretations of beauty have wrought havoc with the female mind. The idea that self-worth, love, success and happiness are directly connected to physical beauty has haunted women, as doggedly as a bloodhound. This daunting idea has often been confirmed by personal experience. From our earliest years, we have either received or seen others receive attention, approval and even affection because of physical beauty.

There was no virtue needed to earn these rewards, no merit or effort required to receive them. No wonder we want, so badly, to be beautiful! Those who *are* beautiful get what they want more often, are loved more by others, and are happier, right?

Some would say, "Of course, right!" The instant popularity of a new TV beauty pageant for ordinary-looking women who undergo plastic surgery, liposuction and dental restoration is built on such worship of physical beauty. And, honestly, deep down inside, don't we all experience a wistful pang when we watch heads turn, mesmerized, as a beautiful woman walks by?

Indeed, every fairytale told during childhood, each story of a heroine or damsel in distress, has endowed its "good" characters with the gift of physical beauty. Songs romanticize and poems idealize the beauty of a woman who is beloved. Even in museums, those impartial bastions of artistic truth, paintings and sculptures idolize a woman's physical beauty.

We seek better skincare and pursue the latest diet trends with frantic fervor, as if our hearts, nerves and minds are drawn, like metal filings, to the magnet of Outer Beauty. For, heaven forefend that, when we walk down the street, we fail to capture the admiration of every man we pass! That would be failure, indeed.

With such an external focus, our reactions become driven by the opinions of others. When we *look* physically superb, alluring and lovely, we *feel* glorious, valued, and worthwhile. Interestingly, when we awaken, tousle-headed and sleepy-eyed, we feel impelled to run for the brush, comb and makeup kit. After all, what woman wants those she hopes to impress to see her unattractive side, "au naturel"?

Don't misunderstand me. I love feeling beautiful, and hope that every woman honors herself by developing her external "beauty potential." Beauty of the body can act as one of the greatest supports for faltering self-esteem. It convinces others that you are confident and, at the same time, without a word spoken, it bolsters your own self-regard.

Yet, when beauty rests solely in the eye of the beholder it is a heavy burden to bear. Pleasing others through the medium of self-adornment costs enormous effort, is transient and reduces our self-esteem to a form of emotional penury, as we beg for a crust of approval here, or a penny of appreciation there.

True beauty, Inner Beauty, is eternal in nature; it is an extension of a healthy mind and spirit. When Inner Beauty is fully developed, physical beauty becomes *its* adornment and is seen and enjoyed, like frosting on a wonderful cake.

Beauty is a state of mind, a choice, part of our spiritual journey toward Inner Beauty. This journey teaches us to blend development of character, through Inner Excellence, with outer harmony of feature, thus nourishing both spirit and body until the eye of the beholder sees us as we see ourselves, beautiful, virtuous and true.

Beauty—A Way of Life

Inner Beauty is the embodiment of spiritual, intellectual and moral excellence. It is an expression of nobility of soul and virtue of character. Inner Beauty enhances Outer Beauty, lending to a woman's features a radiance attainable in no other way.

As we grow in Inner Beauty, we understand the words of Aristotle, when he said, "Excellence is not an act, but a habit."[54] The virtues of Inner Beauty become habitual. We live them effortlessly, unconsciously, until they are as natural as breathing.

Another vital element of our daily Inner Beauty regimen is to focus on the welfare of others, instead of thinking only of ourselves. As we do so, all of the virtues that accompany Inner Excellence will cluster around us. We will become more tender and strong, more virtuous and wise, when we choose the exalted role that combines discipline with nurturing.

As we do this, brightness and warmth enter our daily sphere. We experience beautiful emotions more often, and discover more and more beauty in the world in which we live. "Beauty," Stendhal said, "is the promise of happiness."[55] As our Inner Beauty grows, we become a wellspring of beautiful feelings and choices; we possess a radiance that automatically draws others to us, for refreshment, inspiration and rest.

Beauty and Balance

Our pursuit of Inner Beauty requires incorporating simplicity into our lifestyle to help us achieve greater balance. Yet it is difficult to simplify unless we are clear about what we value. Take some quiet time to think about writing a Values List. Prepare for this activity by clearing your mind of all anxiety and connecting with your feelings, wants and desires.

When you feel relaxed and secure, think about what you value most. Group your values under headings like Family, Education, Talents, Recreation, Social Activities, Hobbies, Self-Development, and so on. And always, always, always write down what you deeply love first and foremost. (Dismiss from your mind responsibilities, duties and tasks that *others* expect you to do. This list is all about what *you* hold precious and dear.)

Once you have mentally defined what matters most, maintain this healthy balance by streamlining your daily activities. Remember to place activities that you value most at the head of your "task list" for the day. This may mean sacrificing superficial activities, like watching television or chattering on the phone. However, as you spend more of your time on what you value, you will experience deeper feelings of happiness, fulfillment and peace.

This is the first step toward bringing greater balance into your life. Your second step is to strip away everything in your environment that is "cluttery." This does not mean throwing out items you treasure. It means selecting the possessions you choose to keep by how well they match your Values List.

Our possessions require care, time and upkeep. Rather than expending energy on what gives us little or no useful or pleasurable return, decide which of your possessions are beautiful, useful or cherished. If they do not fall under one of these three categories, throw them away, give them away or haul them away!

This will "clear the decks," so to speak, for more important matters. If you truly cherish a great many "things" that are not useful, organize them—put them in shelves or storage racks where they can easily be identified and enjoyed. Make certain you "simplify" such items tenderly. The focus here should be to remove what is not valued, while organizing what is loved.

The next step toward simplification is to take charge of your time and just say "No!" Saying "no" up front is a way of honoring self and others. It frees up time, so that you invest your energy in what you value. Learning to say "no" will allow you the liberty to say "yes" to what is truly important.

We have all experienced days when, mired in a jumble of tasks, letters to loved ones and cherished charities received no time or attention. Honestly evaluating what you can and cannot do is one of the best ways to keep your days both simple and satisfying.

The Beauty of Change

Life is fluid and, like water, always flowing. Legend says that you never step into the same river twice. The same thing can be said about life. Each day holds different challenges and rewards. This changeability is beautiful and essential to growth.

Indeed, change is inevitable. Accepting this fact with faith is essential to nourishing our Inner Beauty. Jorge Luis Borges said, "Nothing is built on stone. All is built on sand. But we must build as if the sand were stone." This is a perfect expression of how to face the uncertainty of each day.

Whether we experience changes caused by birth, death, marriage, adoption, divorce, moving or starting a new job, the stress can be enormous. It is normal to re-

spond with deep emotions, some positive, and some nega-
tive. Take heart! There is a way to get through these
situations with grace and you will definitely find it. Your
roadmap is contained within the Seven Virtues.

Remember, the fact that life never stays the same is
what makes it exciting! It may sound trite to say that
what happens to you matters less than how you handle it,
but it's true!

One way to anchor yourself during periods of change,
while increasing your Inner Beauty, is to choose to be-
come your own champion. In the age of *Ivanhoe,* champi-
ons were chosen to fight for the honor of kings, queens
and rulers. Following a few simple steps can help us be-
come our own champions, a healthy approach to dealing
with change.

First, imagine what your ideal champion would be
like. (I don't mean a fighter or knight-errant. I mean a
person handling the situation you now face in a coura-
geous way.) Once you have this picture clearly in mind, go
to your closet and dress like your champion. This may
sound silly, but it really works . . . and is fun as well!

Once you're dressed, step outside and go for a walk.
As you walk, move like your champion, talk like your
champion, feel like your champion. You may laugh a
great deal during this exercise, because these activities
feel like play-acting. Yet this is an extremely effective
way to identify and act upon ideas that will make han-
dling change easier for you.

Now you have one last task to fulfill. It's time for
self-praise. You have just done a wonderful job identify-
ing coping skills for change. Praise yourself. Relax and
put your feet up. Read a book. Call a trustworthy friend
and share your joy. When you reward yourself, after cop-

ing well with change, you make change something you can actually anticipate with enjoyment!

In closing, Ralph Waldo Emerson said, "Though we travel the world over to find the beautiful, we must carry it with us, or we find it not."[56] Remember, every day we "travel" through another twenty-four hours of life. As we trust in our Inner Beauty, each day we experience change with feelings of serenity and peace.

How Inner Attitude Shapes Outer Beauty

Most of us know, instinctively, that the attitudes we hold in our hearts and minds affect how we look. As a model, I saw this repeatedly. We see examples of this around us every day. If you can't recall inner attitude affecting Outer Beauty, take five minutes and walk down a busy sidewalk.

You will see women with common, ordinary features, smiling and radiant, the center of a happy group. You will see women with extraordinary features who may or may not, depending upon their attitudes, enjoy similar happiness and popularity. Our inner attitude affects our Outer Beauty in a big way. However, that's not all it affects.

Attitude also affects opportunity. Whether your attitude is good or bad makes a difference. Attitude is the vehicle that drives either good or bad outcomes in life.

The secret to facing the world with a positive attitude daily is simple, but rarely applied. *You* must focus your thoughts on what you want to do, rather than upon what you have to do.

For example, if I wanted to *lose* weight, it would be tempting to repeat mentally, *I can't eat after 8 P.M. No more sweets or desserts. I must get to the gym, today.* Although these affirmations may sound good, they focus on tasks and limitations. Every time we think *No desserts*, or, *The gym is a must*, we are running from the whip. So let's change the focus and the attitude to what we want, and see what feelings arise.

If we focus on our desires, instead of what we are being denied, affirmations might read like the following. "Exercise gives me the energy to accomplish my goals." "I cherish my body and enjoy eating healthy foods." "I feel better when I eat before 8 P.M." In this second set of affirmations, we are more focused on what we want, rather than upon what we must do. The more we focus on good desires, the more easily and smoothly change occurs. Being grateful for "what is" sustains hope for future goals.

Sustaining a good attitude, regardless of circumstances, is more vital than we know. It is the key to sustaining our progress toward Inner Beauty. This does not mean that we will know why we should have a good attitude. It means just what it says. Have a good attitude no matter what, and you will be enriched.

The following story brings this idea closer to home. Legend states that, many years ago, a teacher was traveling through the Far East with a disciple. After walking through the hills for several days, they saw a small hut on the mountainside. Weak and weary from lack of food, the teacher and the disciple approached the hut.

"Please," the teacher asked the poor farmer, "could you spare us food and shelter for the night?"

"We do not have enough even for ourselves," the poor farmer replied. "My wife and I live on herbs and the little milk we get from our one cow."

The teacher smiled.

"I promise you," he replied, "that if you feed and house us, you will receive something good."

The next morning the farmer returned from his field without milk.

"I am sorry that we can offer you only herbs," he said humbly, to the teacher. "But, during the night, our cow died."

As the teacher and disciple walked away, the disciple turned to the teacher and said, "You promised them something good, but they received a curse. Why?"

"They did not receive a curse!" the teacher replied. "The angel of death came last night for the farmer's wife. But, because the farmer gave us charity, the angel took the spirit of the cow instead."

While this story is a romantic fable, it shows clearly how something that appears to be bad may in actuality be a gift. Remember, keep a good attitude no matter what, and your reward will be an increase of Inner Beauty.

Changing Bad Habits into Beautiful Behavior

"We first make our habits, and then our habits make us.
As the twig is bent, the tree inclines."[57]

—Virgil

Exchanging our bad habits for beautiful behaviors is crucial to sustaining Inner Beauty. This exchange is easier when you treat yourself with dignity and respect. Remember, you are not the sum of your bad habits. You are the total of your positive potential.

When feelings of frustration at the slow pace of change arise, recall the following quote by Mark Twain.

"Bad habits cannot just be thrown out the window,
But, gently coaxed down the stairs, step by step,
And, then, out the door!"[58]

Conclusion

A great deal of my expertise about beauty was acquired during my years as a professional model. I know from personal experience that Outer Beauty has become an industry. Too many women look at magazine covers and say, "Why can't I look like that?" The answer is because nobody looks like that!

As addicted as we are to the glamour of Outer Beauty, Inner Beauty attracts us even more powerfully, with more than color, shape, texture or pattern. It feeds us, with a feast of Inner Excellence based on the Seven Virtues. Although we must spend a certain amount of time daily on Outer Beauty, true and lasting beauty always springs from time spent on Inner Beauty.

Over the years, many people have asked me, "What is your secret to beauty?" In pondering that question, I have recognized that the only secret I know is Inner Beauty.

Life has taught me that each woman is extraordinary, that each woman possesses an Inner Beauty that is independent of makeup, fashion or bone structure—a beauty that may grow to strengthen confidence today and support accomplishments tomorrow. All women have the potential, through application of the Seven Virtues, to create a beauty that shines from within, while influencing future events and transforming their dreams into realities.

If we are honest, we must admit what our hearts have known all along, that Inner Beauty is so magnetic, so attractive, that we admire whoever possesses it and often try to emulate them by increasing our Outer Beauty. Nonetheless, our fascination with Inner Beauty runs deep. It is the fire that makes women who possess it examples in life, and immortals in memory.

There is a treasured part of each of us that we must keep hidden. This preciousness is the personal secret to our own Inner Beauty. As we give time and attention to this uniqueness, our Inner Beauty grows and we reap its rewards.

A woman with Inner Beauty possesses the power to lead by joyous example. A woman with Inner Beauty holds in her heart the golden secret to a happy life.

*   *   *

End Notes

1. Cahill, Gloria. "This Designing Woman Gives the Fashion Industry a Reality Check." *Radiance Magazine*. Fall 1997. (http://www.radiancemagazine.com/delta.html).

2. Ibid.

3. Ibid.

4. Payne, January W. "Beyond Appearances. Anorexia's Cause: Not Just Body Dissatisfaction," *The Washington Post*. July 6, 2004. (http://www.washingtonpost.com/wp-dyn/articles/A29786-2004Jul5.html).

5. Randazzo, Sal. *The Myth Makers: How Advertisers Apply the Power of Classic Myths & Symbols to Create Modern Day Legends*. Chicago, IL: Probus Publishing, 1995.

6. Stewart, Mary. *Moon-Spinners*. Greenwich, Conn: Fawcett Publications, 1963.

7. Emerson, Ralph Waldo. *The Rhodora*. Emerson Central. August 10, 2004. http://www.emersoncentral.com/poems/rhodora.htm.

8. *Dictionary.com*. 2004. http://dictionary.reference.com/search?q=Beauty.

9. Ibid.

10. *History of the Taj Mahal*. The World of Royalty website. http://www.royalty.nu/Asia/India/TajMahal.html

11. Ibid.

12. Ibid.

13. *History of the Taj Mahal*. Taj Mahal: The Monument of Love site. Indiaserver.com. http://www.tajmahalindia.net/history-of-taj-mahal.html.

14. Shoffstall, Veronnica A. *After A While*. Comes the Dawn: About Healing After Divorce. June 26, 2004. My Divorce Recovery site. http://home.att.net/~velvet-hammer/comesthedawn.html.

15. "Wherever You Are—Be There." Life Excellence Newsletter, January 25, 2002. Lifeexcellence.com.

16. Matthew 7:6. *King James Bible*. Salt Lake City, UT: Deseret Book Company.

17. "In Beauty May I Walk." A Navajo Poem. Translatum: the Greek

Translation Vortal. 2004. Translatumgr. http://www.translatum.gr/poetry/navajo.html.

18. *Rise of the Phoenix.* Mythical Realm. 2004. Lady Gryphon's Mythical Realm. http://www.mythicalrealm.com/creatures/phoenix.html.

19. *Aristotle Quotes.* Quote of the Day. 2004. http://www.brainyquote.com/quotes/quotes/a/aristotle117836.html.

20. *A Free Essay on Ancient Greek Fashions.* Essaycrawler.com. http://www.essaycrawler.com/viewpaper/35048.html.

21. *A Brief History of Fashion.* Eras of Elegance, Inc. 2000-2003. Erasofelegance.com. http://www.erasofelegance.com/fashion4.html.

22. Marshall, Suzanne G. *Individuality in Clothing Selection & Personal Appearance.* 5th Edition. Upper Saddle River, NJ: Prentice Hall Inc., 2000.

23. *The Navajo Night Way Ceremony. Translated by Rothenberg, Jerome K.* Feb. 18, 2000. http://www.cs.rice.edu/~ssiyer/minstrels/poems/344.html.

24. Shakespeare, William. "Sonnet 1." *The Complete Illustrated Shakespeare.* Park Lane, NY: Crown Publishers, Inc., 1979.

25. *Quotations by Subject.* Quotations Page and Michael Moncour. July 2002. http://www.quotationspage.com/subjects/perfection/.

26. *Quotations on Beauty.* RavenZcry. 1999. Lady Raven. http://www.geocities.com/Paris/Arc/4941/qbeauty.html.

27. *Rise of the Phoenix.* Mythical Realm. 2004, Lady Gryphon's Mythical Realm. http://www.mythicalrealm.com/creatures/phoenix.html.

28. Pickford, Kaylan. *Always Beautiful.* New York : Putnam, 1985.

29. Smith, Marizio G. "American Indian Vision Quest." *Sunrise Magazine,* October/November 1986. Theosophical University Press. http://www.theosophy-nw.org/theosnw/world/america/am-smit.htm.

30. *Elizabeth Kubler-Ross Quotes.* Quote of the Day. 2004. Brainyquotes. http://www.brainyquote.com/quotes/quotes/e/elisabethk 119810.html.

31. Tore Frangsmyr and Irwin Abrams, eds. *Nobel Lectures, Peace 1971–1980.* Singapore: World Scientific Publishing Co., 1997. http://www.nobel.se/peace/laureates/1979/teresa-bio.html.

32. Louisa May Alcott—Biography. *Empire:Zine.* Credit Source: Camden County Free Library. Voorhees, NJ. Spyder's Empire. August 17, 2004. http://www.empirezine.com/spotlight/alcott/alcott.htm.

33. Anne Sullivan Macy. American Foundation for the Blind. http://www.afb.org/section.asp?Documentid=927.
34. "Tragedy to Triumph: An Adventure with Helen Keller." *In Search of the Heroes.* © 1995 Grace Products Corporation. http://www.graceproducts.com/keller/anne.html.
35. Maria Sklodowska-Curie. 1867–1934. Zb.Zwolinski, ed. http://hum.amu.edu.pl/~zbzw/ph/sci/msc.htm.
36. corpinfo@rnib.org.uk. *The Life of Helen Keller.* RNIB—Helping You Live with Sight Loss. Royal National Institute of the Blind. http://www.rnib.org.uk/xpedio/groups/public/documents/publicwebsite/public_keller.hcsp.
37. Gibson, William. *The Miracle Worker.* William Gibson. 1962.
38. *The Life of Helen Keller.* American Foundation for the Blind. Web101hosting.com. http://www.sapphyr.net/women/helenkeller.htm.
39. Henney, Nella. *Helen Keller Visits Eaton.* Conway Public Library. The Reporter, North Conway, NH. http://www.conway.lib.nh.us/history/keller.htm.
40. corpinfo@rnib.org.uk. *The Life of Helen Keller.* RNIB—Helping You Live with Sight Loss. Royal National Institute of the Blind. http://www.rnib.org.uk/xpedio/groups/public/documents/publicwebsite/public_keller.hcsp.
41. *The Life of Helen Keller.* American Foundation for the Blind. Web101hosting.com. http://www.sapphyr.net/women/helenkeller.htm.
42. *Anne Frank Biography.* Utahlink. http://www.uen.org/utahlink/lp_res/AnneFrankBioShort.html.
43. Anne Frank—An Unfinished Story. Anne Frank—the Writer (Launch the Exhibition). US Holocaust Memorial Museum. Copyright © United States Holocaust Memorial Museum, Washington, D.C. August 17, 2004.
44. Ibid.
45. *Anne Frank Introductory Quote.* Anne Frank Center USA. News Editor—Steve Frank. Anne Frank Online. August 17, 2004. http://www.annefrank.com/.
46. *General US Statistic Sites.* The Reference Desk Statistics. December 18, 2003. Davenport Public Library. August 17, 2004. http://www.rbls.lib.il.us/dpl/ref/topics/refstats.htm.
47. *Life Depends on You.* Quote of the Day—May 24, 2004. Coolpup.com. http://www.dailycelebrations.com/052400.htm.
48. *St. Augustine Quotes.* BrainyQuotes. http://www.brainyquote.com/quotes/authors/s/saint_augustine.html.
49. *Mother Teresa.* Pearls of Wisdom. Web101hosting.com. http://www.sapphyr.net/women/motherteresa.htm.

50. *Quotes by Grant M. Bright.* Self-Esteem. Bright Quotes. March 3, 2003. Grant Bright. http://pw1.netcom.com/~spritex/self_est.html.
51. *Letter to Theo.* Apple Seeds. May 2000. Apple Seeds Archives. http://www.appleseeds.org/May_2000.htm.
52. *Kahlil Gibran on Beauty.* Anyara-Aphorisms. 2001–2004. Beauty Quotations. http://koti.mbnet.fi/neptunia/authors/gibran61.htm.
53. *Beauty.* Quote Me On It. http://www.quotemeonit.com/beauty.html.
54. *A Select Collection of Excellence Quotes.* Excellence Quote. 2004. A PRIMEDIA Co. http://quotations.about.com/cs/inspiration quotes/a/Excellence1.htm.
55. *Beauty.* Quotes to Inspire You. Cyber Nation International, Inc.1999.http://www.cyber-nation.com/victory/quotations/subjects/quotes_beauty.html.
56. *Beauty.* Quoteland.com. 1997–2001 http://www.quoteland.com/author.asp?AUTHOR_ID=5.
57. *Miller, Emmett, MD.* Self-Healing Products. http://www.drmiller.com/products/behavior.html.
58. Ibid.

114